My Neighbor
Saw Me Naked

and Other Reasons
You Need Drapes

My Neighbor Saw Me Naked

and Other Reasons You Need Drapes

THE ESSENTIAL DECORATING HANDBOOK

Annie Elliott

Illustrations by Tania Lee

ARTISAN | NEW YORK

Library of Congress Cataloging-in-Publication Data is on file.

ISBN 978-1-64829-470-9

Design by Rae Ann Spitzenberger
Cover illustration by Tania Lee
Chapter opener patterns by Ying Cheng
Endpapers and page 6: Textile Artwork/Shutterstock

Artisan books may be purchased in bulk for business, educational, or promotional
use. For information, please contact your local bookseller or the Hachette Book
Group Special Markets Department at special.markets@hbgusa.com.

The publisher is not responsible for websites (or their content) that are not
owned by the publisher.

The Hachette Speakers Bureau provides a wide range of authors for speaking
events. To find out more, go to hachettespeakersbureau.com or email
HachetteSpeakers@hbgusa.com.

Published by Artisan,
an imprint of Workman Publishing,
a division of Hachette Book Group, Inc.
1290 Avenue of the Americas
New York, NY 10104
artisanbooks.com

The Artisan name and logo are registered trademarks of Hachette Book Group, Inc.

Printed in China (APS) on responsibly sourced paper

First printing, July 2025

10 9 8 7 6 5 4 3 2 1

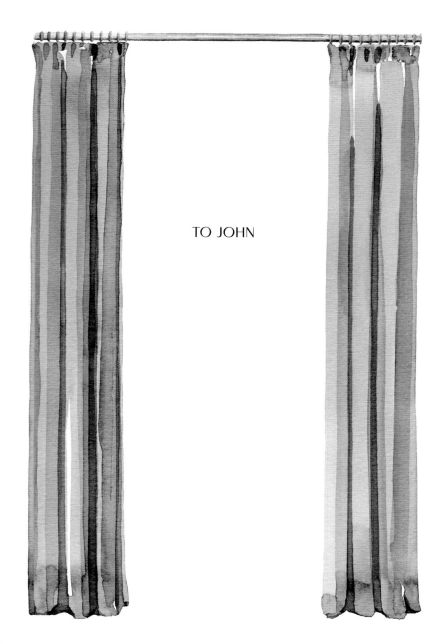

TO JOHN

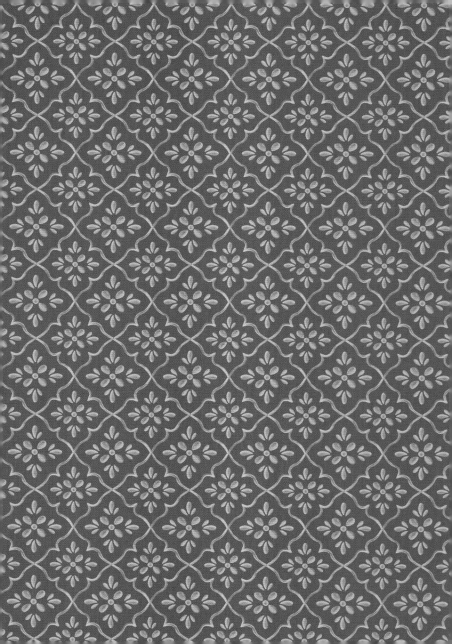

CONTENTS

INTRODUCTION

Does the world really need another book about interior design?

Yes, Gentle Reader. It does. Or rather, it needs *this* book. Because while there exist dozens—nay, hundreds!—of gorgeous coffee-table books with stunning pictures of country estates and urban penthouses, and oodles of DIY books that promise domiciliary bliss via chalk paint and fusible bonding web, there is no book that gives it to you straight. No book that provides only the *most* important things you need to know as you feather your nest. The bottom-line advice.

In my twenty-plus years running an interior design business, I have collected, like a magpie, shiny little nuggets of wisdom. Nuggets such as a large room requires a lamp that's around 30 inches tall, and 8 by 10 feet may be too small for a dining room rug. Should these tidbits simply float in the ether, to be learned by decorating enthusiasts through painstaking trial and error? Or should they be compiled, written down in black and white by an expert, so they may prevent said enthusiasts from wasting precious time and money and making decisions they will regret?

I say the latter.

I didn't start my working life as an interior decorator.[1] While I'd always been interested in beautiful houses and the objects with which we choose to live, I thought I was destined to become a museum director. After college, I worked at the Rosenbach Museum & Library in Philadelphia, where my office was a maid's room on the fourth floor of a nineteenth-century townhouse. Heaven! After three years, my director

---

[1] A terminology clarification: Most people use "interior designer" and "interior decorator" interchangeably. Technically, interior designers have a degree in interior design and a license permitting them to produce construction drawings. Therefore, self-educated design professionals such as Jonathan Adler, Barbara Barry, and Nate Berkus technically are interior decorators. As am I.

told me to go to graduate school or he'd fire me, so I headed to the institution with the weightiest name I could find: the Williams College Graduate Program in the History of Art.

During my time at Williams, I learned a great deal about art history (of course), but my big takeaway was learning how to *look* at art: You take your time. You stare. You think about scale, balance, and proportion: How do shapes relate to each other? What's the rhythm of objects across a canvas? How do colors work together—or against one another—to communicate a message or create a mood? How does a piece of art interact with the viewer? Although I eventually replaced my dream of becoming a museum director with that of becoming an interior designer, the principles I learned in graduate school still apply.

So what exactly *did* prompt the switch from museum worker to intrepid interior designer-slash-decorator? As much as I loved art and museums, living in D.C. after graduate school, I realized that I was most passionate about people's *relationship* to art—and, by extension, people's relationship to their surroundings. I'd worked in museums for ten years. Would it be crazy to start a new career at this stage of life (especially since I was pregnant with twins)? To test the waters, I enrolled in some design classes while working at the Corcoran Gallery of Art, and I received just enough encouragement to make me think that a career in design might be possible.

Then, a fateful evening. My husband and I had some friends over for dinner. We had just finished renovating our postage stamp–size kitchen, and they loved it. They were beginning a major renovation of their Capitol Hill house and asked me to join their architect and contractor as part of the design team. And so my fledgling design business was born. I put out the word that I was considering a career change, and my friends started calling. "Can you help me figure out where my furniture will go in my new apartment?" "I don't know if my rug is working. Take a look?" And "Help! The painters are coming on Thursday!" Actually, I still get that last one.

On the business side, let's just say I became something of an expert at reinventing the wheel. Writing client contracts, paint schedules, fabric orders . . . I was *really* winging it. But wing it I did. Twenty years later, I have systems in place to afford me the privilege of making people happy by transforming their homes into places that gratify, delight, and inspire.

And now I hope I can do the same for you, albeit in a smaller way. This handbook provides answers to the questions that undoubtedly will arise as you create the home of your dreams. Questions such as *How large should my rug be? Where should I hang wallpaper? How do I style an empty tabletop?* And, of course, *Do I really need window treatments?* You'll have me in your pocket, at the ready with clear answers to your trickiest design challenges. I've even included a list of helpful dimensions—a cheat sheet, if you will—at the end of this book for quick reference. Clip 'n' save if you so desire.

Read on, Gentle Reader. Read on.

1

WINDOW TREATMENTS

Yes, you need *something*
on your windows

Does this subject really deserve top billing? After an unfortunate incident, I must say that I believe it does.

I was in our bathroom, air-drying après-shower, and I turned to grab my hairbrush. As I was pivoting, I glanced out the window, and my neighbor across the alley was standing at *his* window, just looking at me. And do you know what he did, Gentle Reader? He *waved*.

Window treatments[1] are necessary for two reasons: privacy—whether you think you need it or not—and light control.

....

[1] As desperately as I wish this term described the psychiatric help your windows might require, it does not. "Window treatment" simply refers to any covering you put on an interior window: drapes, curtains, shades, shutters, etc.

PRIVACY

Most of us know instinctively that in bedrooms and bathrooms, window treatments are essential unless you're equally body-confident and magnanimous. We're less convinced when it comes to the more public rooms in your house.

Let's say you have beautiful multipaned windows in your family room. You may think privacy is not an issue because the room is at the back of the house, overlooking a large garden, with nary a neighbor in sight. You want an unobstructed view of that beautiful garden, and you want to let in as much light as possible. I understand! How lovely to look out onto a large green expanse on a bright summer day!

But when the sun goes down and the windows turn dark, your beautiful view is replaced by black holes. Black holes that function as mirrors in which you and your surroundings are reflected. Don't you feel a bit . . . exposed? While there probably *isn't* anyone looking in your windows, it feels as though there could be. And don't forget that many trees lose leaves in winter. Gardens we assume are private in the lush months may be less so when the seasons change.

Don't take my word for it. Around seven o'clock on a February evening, leave someone in your fully lit family room and take the dog for a walk across the back of the house. How much can you see? Everything.

LIGHT CONTROL

When it comes to light control, there are three levels of opacity from which to choose.

The most extreme is blackout, examples of which are solid interior shutters and curtains with a triple lining. Many people opt for blackout treatments in bedrooms, especially nurseries. I personally find blackout shades disorienting, but I believe I am in the minority.

To dim sunlight but stop short of complete darkness, a privacy lining is a standard option for drapes and Roman shades. This thin cotton lining (like muslin) darkens a room but doesn't block 100 percent of the light.

Then there are situations in which simply filtering the light is desirable. If, one morning, you bring your laptop into your east-facing dining room and rays of sunlight are shining directly into your eyes (for example), semi-sheer drapes or curtains will cut the glare just enough for you to go about your business.

TYPES OF WINDOW TREATMENTS

Drapes and Curtains

People use these terms interchangeably, but I say "drapes" when referring to floor-length panels and "curtains" for treatments that are shorter—say, windowsill length. I use drapes in formal or "public" spaces (such as living rooms and dining rooms) and in adults' bedrooms, and I generally use curtains in children's bedrooms. Curtains are lighthearted and informal, so that's where they belong.

As for functionality, it doesn't get simpler than drapes and curtains. During the day, panels may be pushed totally clear of the windows, allowing light to stream through, and at night, they're drawn for privacy and coziness. As a bonus, drapes (due to their length) are especially great insulators in drafty houses. There are many details to consider when it comes to choosing drapery; for more information, see page 25.

Roman Shades

Another terrific window treatment option is Roman shades: flat panels that can be raised and lowered. These provide a tailored look and are perfect in small rooms that cannot accommodate the volume of drapes. They may be installed inside the window trim, on the trim itself, or on the wall above the window frame. I hear you asking, so allow me to preempt your question: If you mount the Roman shades inside the window frame, yes, you *will* lose 6 to 8 inches of windowpane at the very top when the shades are pulled up. I promise, however, that your view will not be obstructed significantly. If you really, really don't want to cover even a sliver of glass, you can mount the shades high on the wall, almost at the crown moulding. You may cover a tiny bit of your pretty woodwork even when the shades are raised all the way, but you can't have everything.

Roman shades don't have to be fabric. Another tasteful type to consider is natural woven Roman shades, which are made of bamboo or natural grasses.

Roman shades

natural woven Roman shades

drapes & valance

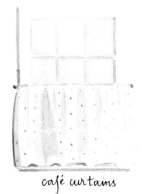

café curtains

shutters
(small slats _only_)

Another excellent option for half coverage is café curtains. I am going to start calling these, simply, "short curtains," because we all think of a French bistro when we hear "café curtains," don't we? Au contraire, mon frère! Café curtains can be quite elegant! Keep the rods and rings small and, as with the shutters, mount them just above the window's sash lock. The fabric should be semi-sheer to provide privacy *and* a glow from the sun. I use café curtains—excuse me, short curtains—often, especially on staircase landings and in powder rooms.

I would be remiss if I didn't mention the "top-down/bottom-up" style, which, as the clunky name suggests, can be adjusted to cover only the bottom half of a window. It's an option for Roman shades and pleated or cell shades, but I'm afraid I cannot recommend it. First of all, this type of treatment is prone to breakage. Second, you are forced to have a valance at the top to disguise the up/down mechanism, which is not pretty. Third, and most egregiously, rows of strings are visible whether the treatment is half up or half down. Tight strings and dangly strings. Lots of strings.

Other Window Treatment Options

Falling into the category of "possible only under special, decorator-supervised circumstances" are fabric-y roller shades, cellular shades, and solar shades. When I use any of these, it's usually as a first layer under Roman shades or drapes.

Never advisable are plastic roller shades, vertical blinds, and café curtains *with a valance*.

DRAPES: A PRIMER

Because drapes are among the most common window treatments and have more variables to consider than other types (*What kind of pleats, if any? What length? What size and color drapery rod, and where does it go?*), it's worth returning to the topic for a moment.

Versatile and elegant, drapes offer options for every space and style. Semi-sheer linen drapes, for example, are lovely in both traditional and modern settings. For super-contemporary interiors, ripple-fold, lightweight drapes hung from a ceiling track are simple and appropriate, so I'm afraid I must reject the excuse that a home is simply "too modern for

ACCEPTABLE

kiss the floor

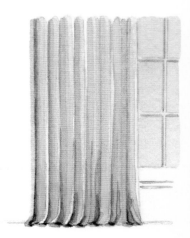

break

ILL-ADVISED

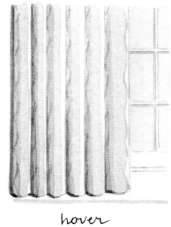

hover

puddle

window treatments." Here is some information to guide you as you navigate the oft-confusing world of drapery.

Length

I like drapes that just "kiss the floor," as my fabricator says. Some people prefer them to "break" like a gentleman's trousers. I don't love this, but I can live with it. If your drapery fabric is fairly thick, it will stretch slightly after a few months. In that case, you either can re-pin the drapes to bring them up a hair, or you can decide that you like the break and leave the drapes alone.

There are two things that drapes should *not* do: They should not hover over the floor by an inch or more. You know when a little boy has had a growth spurt and his pants become "floods"? It's like that. And they definitely should not bunch up on the floor, which is called "puddling." I don't care if some decorators declare that puddling is in vogue again. It looks messy and careless.

Headers

This term refers to the top of drapery panels, where they attach to a rod or track. There are many options, but you can't go wrong with a simple pinch pleat (two folds).[2]

"Rod-pocket" headers, in which a drapery rod is pushed through a channel at the top of a panel, look . . . how can I say this? . . . cheap. And they're not functional: It's nearly impossible for drapes to stay open when they have a rod-pocket header.

Finally, please avoid "grommet" headers. (Those are the ones with huge, metal-ringed holes punched through the fabric, allowing the rod to weave through.) They're inelegant and clunky.

Hardware

When it comes to mounting drapery hardware, high and wide is the order of the day. I recommend installing the drapery rod approximately halfway between the top of the window moulding and the ceiling—you

[2] Confusingly, these can also be called "continental pleats" or, less often, "French pleats."

can go all the way to the ceiling if you like. If possible, extend the rods 4 to 8 inches to the right and left of the window frame so the drapes cover less of the glass. This makes the window appear larger, and the drapes will obstruct less of the view.

If you opt for a valance (a wide strip of fabric across the top of a window, over the top of the drapes), you eliminate the need for rods and rings. The valance hides the less attractive operational hardware. My favorite type of valances are "tailored"—a simple flat style with pleats at the corners.

CUSTOM WINDOW TREATMENTS

I'm saving the most painful truth for last: Custom window treatments, especially fabric ones, are expensive. But from a decorating standpoint, you will not make a better investment. Nothing off-the-shelf will look as lovely and purposeful. They will fit, they will coordinate with the rest of the room, and they will make your home feel complete. Please invest in custom window treatments the minute you move into a new home so you can enjoy them for as long as possible.

2

RUGS

Yours are probably
too small

Rugs[1] are quite literally the foundation of every room. It's important to get them right. The size of the rug, the size of the pattern, what materials are used, the overall design . . . there are many things to consider.

....

[1] On "carpet" versus "rug": There's no difference, really. I tend to say "rug" for a floor covering that comes in predetermined sizes. I say "carpet*ing*" when I'm referring to broadloom, which is what you use for stair runners, wall-to-wall carpeting, and custom-cut rugs. Now that I think about it, I almost never say "carpet." There's nothing wrong with it; I just don't say it.

RUG SIZE

Unless your rugs are crawling up the baseboards, they're not too big. Large rugs make a room look bigger, and they protect your beautiful floors from scratches and sunlight. (If your floors *aren't* beautiful, rugs hide them, of course.) If a room can accommodate a large rug, please consider that option first.

In a living room or family room, all furniture in a conversation area ideally will fit onto the rug. If that's not possible, try placing the rug in front of the sofa but under the chairs opposite or adjacent. It doesn't look great when *every* piece of furniture is half-on, half-off the rug. In dining rooms, the chairs must be able to move around without catching their legs on the rug. This means that most of the time, an 8-by-10-foot rug is too small for a dining room. A 9-by-12-foot or even 10-by-14-foot option may be better.

Having just made the case for large rugs, I will take a moment to acknowledge that many of us already have a small rug or two—and by "small" I mean 5 by 7 feet or smaller. Ideally, of course, you'd simply place a small rug in a small space, such as a foyer, a small bedroom, or a hallway. If you're determined to use a small rug in a larger area, however, it's going to look lonely floating in the middle of a bare floor, so place it on top of a room-size seagrass, sisal, or wool flatweave rug. The first layer will fill out the space, and the small rug on top will anchor the area in which it is laid (ideally, the conversation area). Plush cut-pile or large-looped rugs do not make a good first layer, because the smaller rug on top will kick up and buckle unattractively (and unsafely).

Layering an assortment of small-to-medium rugs is a charming option if you like an informal, bohemian vibe. Use three or more so your design looks intentional, and it's best to keep the rugs the same type—all vintage or all cotton flatweaves, for example. One benefit of layering rugs is that you can cover as much or as little of the floor as you like, and you can get into the nooks and crannies of an oddly shaped room.

Here's another trick if your room isn't perfectly rectangular or square (or has a fireplace or a bay window): custom-cut broadloom carpeting that follows a room's perimeter. A safe bet is to leave 2 to 3 inches

carpeting cut
to contour
of room

layered
rugs

of floor visible around the edges (the "reveal"). As an example, a client had a long, skinny living room with a gas fireplace in the middle. Rather than chop up the room with a series of small rugs, we installed bound broadloom carpeting that left 3 inches of floor exposed all the way around the room—except for around the hearth, where we reduced the exposed floor to 2 inches. It's beautiful, and it unifies the room in a considered way.

RUG CONTENT

Wool

If durability is a priority, go with wool. Wool rugs are generally considered the hardiest and easiest to clean. Some—not all—industry professionals insist that nylon cleans the best. I respectfully disagree. Wool has natural oils, such as lanolin, which protect the fibers and repel stains. Plus it's just nicer. (Don't leave a spill sitting on a wool rug overnight, of course, but if you act quickly, you will avoid a stain.)

There are more inexpensive wool rugs and broadloom on the market than ever before, so please don't let cost be a deterrent until you've done some shopping. Definitely go with wool for stair runners if you can, as it stands up best to heavy wear. And most of the cost of stair runners is in the labor—the templating, edge binding, and installation. (Do keep in mind, however, that while wool is easy to clean, it is a brave—or naïve—person who installs a white stair runner.)

Plant Fibers

This category consists of seagrass, sisal, and jute. I love all of them, but they're not interchangeable. Seagrass is the most durable and stain-resistant of all the plant fibers. It's terrific for foyers and mudrooms, and as a first layer under smaller rugs. If you can get your hands on a decent-size sample, be sure to walk on it in bare feet before committing. I *love* the feel—as a bonus, seagrass exfoliates!—but some people find its coarseness unpleasant. Sisal is pretty tough, and, like seagrass, it makes for a great first layer under a smaller rug. It stains easily, though. The softest of the natural plant fiber rugs, jute holds stains and doesn't wear particularly well. It is, however, perfect for bedrooms.

Nylon

As acknowledged previously, nylon *is* stain-resistant, but it won't wear as well as wool. Over time (I'm talking years, not months), wool in a heavily trafficked area will wear away rather charmingly. Plush nylon, on the other hand, flattens and looks like a Muppet run over by a car. I learned this the hard way.

Cotton

Cotton dhurries[2] look so fresh and summery . . . who doesn't love a striped cotton runner on a beach house staircase? But cotton grabs dirt and won't let go. I strongly advise against cotton rugs if you have pets or children. And if you drink red wine, forget it.

-----

[2] Casual flatweave rugs.

RUG STYLES

Antique

It used to be that people in their thirties and younger would roll their eyes when you mentioned Persian, Turkish, or other heavily patterned, handmade antique rugs. Thanks to the rise of bohemian and maximalist styles, however, vintage and antique rugs have undergone a rise in popularity. Hooray!

I have *always* been a huge fan. There are many reasons: First, antique rugs are surprisingly versatile. They look fantastic in traditional interiors, of course (make sure you have a few modern pieces of furniture to balance things out), but the contrast of such a rug in an architecturally sleek space is equally smashing. Second, antique rugs show *nothing*, so if you have young children or willful pets, they're perfect. Third, they're easily attainable. If your great-aunt hasn't given you one already, you may be able to snap up a large vintage rug on eBay or Craigslist for an incredibly reasonable price. My dining room rug cost—wait for it—less than $300! Including shipping! That may have been a once-in-a-lifetime find, but you get my point.

Solid

Rugs in a solid, light to medium, neutral color (e.g., ivory, beige, or gray) are infinitely popular and perfectly fine. They work in every context: city or country, traditional or contemporary, colorful or subdued. I do prefer solid-colored rugs to have a bit of a fleck (as is often the case with rugs described as "oatmeal"), a pattern in the weave, or some "carving" so there are variations in pile height. *Something* to break up the expanse.

Surprisingly, it can be difficult to decorate with solid-colored rugs and wall-to-wall carpeting that are *not* a light neutral. Instead of giving you lots of colors to pull from (like an antique patterned rug) or making no statement at all (like a solid neutral rug), a solid-colored rug (say, red or dark green) becomes an attention-grabbing block of color in a room. (Additional points taken away if the rug is a nylon plush pile.) Let me be clear: I am talking about *solid* solid colors: no fleck, no strié, no color variation whatsoever. The only acceptable kind of solid-colored rug is a Gabbeh, a thick, handmade Persian rug in a rich vegetable dye. Some Gabbehs have large patterns (some merely have depictions of people or animals woven into the corners), but even the solid ones are cheerful and fun.

Two-Tone Geometric

When the pattern is small, a two-tone rug can be the solution to many a decorating dilemma, especially when you have a vast expanse of floor to cover. Ivory or white is usually one of the colors: Picture a blue-and-white wool flatweave or a gray-and-ivory cut-pile rug in a herringbone pattern. Two-tone rugs are versatile and infinitely more interesting than those in solid colors.

Striped

Here's the secret: The wider the stripe, the less formal the feel. A wool flatweave with broad red-and-white stripes (say 8 inches wide) would be darling in a child's bedroom, wouldn't it? A multicolor rug with pencil-wide stripes would be perfect in a family room. And when its stripes are reduced to a tiny strié pattern, a striped rug is beautiful in even the most formal living room.

Animal Print

Rugs with an animal print such as zebra or antelope are classic and infinitely elegant. I placed a needlepoint-like small cheetah pattern (in ivory, beige, and black) in a client's formal dining room, and it looks absolutely gorgeous—and cheeky to boot.

Large-Scale Designs

Do not concern yourself with rugs that have extremely large, uncentered botanical or geometric shapes. They're impossible. Rugs like this dominate whatever room they occupy, sucking the life out of everything in their orbit: furniture, wallpaper, artwork, and inhabitants.

RUG PADS

Rug pads are essential. Not only do they keep small rugs (and therefore people) from sliding around, they also prevent damage to your floors. Over time, a tightly knotted rug acts like fine-grit sandpaper, gradually wearing away your floor finish. Who knew?!

Rubbery waffle-weave rug pads work for tiny rugs, but if they're not replaced every few years, the pads may stick to the floor (leaving a residue) or dry out and crumble. In general, I prefer thick felt rug pads with a rubber backing. In addition to preventing slips *and* protecting your floors, rugs over felt pads feel delightfully cushy underfoot. Even if your rug is so large that it's held down by multiple pieces of furniture, please do yourself and your floors the favor of installing a rug pad.

WALL-TO-WALL CARPETING

Wall-to-wall carpeting can make a room feel wonderfully cozy, which is why it's beloved in bedrooms and chilly basement playrooms. Wall-to-wall carpeting in formal living spaces is uncommon right now, but it wasn't always thus. The legendary decorator Billy Baldwin adored wall-to-wall carpeting for living rooms—especially in white. Brave!

Surprisingly, wall-to-wall carpeting can be less expensive than custom-cut broadloom (discussed on page 34). The cost of binding broadloom easily outweighs the cost of the extra carpeting required for a wall-to-wall installation.

PURCHASING RUGS

Carpeting and rugs are extremely difficult to envision from a photo of a room in a catalog or, worse, a postage stamp–size picture on a website. There's no better way to get a true feel for a rug's colors and the scale of the pattern than by seeing it in person.

Actually, the *very* best is being able to see the rug in your home. Independent rug sellers often are willing to let you borrow a rug "on approval" to see if you like it in your space. There may be a small delivery fee, but it will be money well spent. Having the unrolled rug in the room for even a few minutes (as the delivery person taps their foot waiting for a decision) is helpful. You usually know instantly if the rug works.

All of that said, I recognize that it isn't always possible to see our dream floor covering physically before purchasing it. But returning a full-size rug is a pain in the neck, so if you need a specific color (a cherry red rather than an orangey red, for example), it's worth the time and money to pay for a sample or order the 2-by-3-foot size and plan to return it.

Unfortunately, this is an option only in the case of new, mass-produced rugs.

Purchasing a one-of-a-kind rug online is especially risky, in part because the sellers may not use the highest-quality photographs in their advertisements. You have no way of knowing what the colors *actually* look like until you have the rug in your hot little hands. (I've seen one seller photograph Pantone color chips alongside the rugs, which is genius. More vendors should adopt this practice.) I'm most willing to order sight unseen when a room's color palette is somewhat flexible. I once ordered a small rug that was described as "sage green" but was decidedly brown. It was fine in that particular case, but if I'd *really* needed sage, I'd have been out of luck.

3

FURNITURE

Narrow arms, slender legs,
and tight seats

Oh, Gentle Reader. How I wish with all my heart that I could impart hard-and-fast rules for selecting and arranging furniture. Alas, they do not exist. The minute I think of a guideline or principle, two exceptions spring to mind. That said, I hope the following information is useful.

The most important things to consider when purchasing a piece of furniture—be it an upholstered piece or a case good[1]—are size and scale. *Size* so that you may be sure the piece is the proper *scale* for the room in which it will be placed. It must be in harmony with the space and the other furniture in it. The following pages include some size guidelines for general categories of furniture.

....

[1] A non-upholstered piece of furniture that provides interior storage space, such as a cabinet or bookcase. But many people, including yours truly, apply the term to any wooden piece of furniture.

LIVING ROOM FURNITURE

Sofas

A large room with a tall ceiling calls for a correspondingly large sofa: say, a minimum of 84 inches wide[2] and 38 inches deep, with a back at least 34 inches high. (Beware: Many furniture manufacturers describe the overall height of a piece as the distance from floor to "rail," which is the frame of the sofa. You see the problem—most sofas have back cushions that extend up past the rail. Please take back cushions into account when measuring the height of a sofa.) When you have a big room, get as deep a sofa as is comfortable for you. Thirty-eight inches is a universally comfortable depth (accent pillows were invented for the vertically challenged, like me, whose feet may not hit the floor otherwise), with a 44-inch depth becoming increasingly common.

Large sofas tend to have loose seat and back cushions, which are exactly what they sound like: cushions

....

[2] Another terminology clarification: Some manufacturers refer to a side-to-side dimension as "length" and front to back as "width." I, however, have always used "width" for side to side and "depth" for front to back.

that can be removed for fluffing and cleaning. (When you have a single seat cushion, that's called a "bench seat." I love the look, but be warned that the cushion will wear unevenly: It will mush down in the center more quickly than at the sides. A three-cushion sofa will retain its firmness better.)

Alternatively, when space is at a premium, the size of your sofa matters quite a bit. Many retailers now offer "apartment sofas" that are shorter than 72 inches (I defy you to explain how they differ from "loveseats"), but finding shallower depths remains a challenge. Your modest room may require a sofa that is 33 inches deep maximum, which is tricky to find. But do not lose heart! Look for sofas that have "tight" backs (no back cushions), because tight-back sofas tend to be on the shallower side. I find them to be quite comfy, but if you desire loungey-ness, mushy accent pillows are your best friends. (More about those in Chapter 7.)

In extremely small rooms, sometimes a sofa that fits physically may not be successful aesthetically. The proportions must be petite to work visually in the space: Narrow arms; slender, exposed legs; and a low back will make a sofa appear less weighty. Add a tight seat and tight back to the equation and your sofa becomes a settee. These work in the smallest of spaces, including, sometimes, staircase landings.

A quick note about sectionals: Unless all sides of the sectional have a back (no chaises, in other words), you're not necessarily increasing your seating capacity. And you must have end tables when you have a sectional, as the round coffee table that fits so neatly into the crook is not reachable by all.

Chairs

As with sofas, upholstered lounge chairs should reflect the size of the room in which they are placed: large room, large chair; small room, smaller chair. Depth is an especially important consideration for lounge chairs, as they may be "floating" on either side of a sofa. In a normal-size room, if those chairs are 36 inches deep, they are going to take up a *lot* of visual and actual space—they may even look too heavy for the sofa. Chairs that are 30 inches deep are less likely to dominate.

Not every chair in a living or family room must be upholstered. Lighter chairs such as a wooden Windsor or an acrylic Ghost chair are called "occasional chairs," and they're meant to be pulled into the conversation area as needed and pushed away when the party's over. While comfort is a bonus, it's not critical. You may prioritize form over function for your extra seating, as no one will be relegated to these perches forever. Beautiful objects first, practical seating second.

A word about swivel chairs: They can be useful, but if you are a person who likes things *just so*, a person who straightens pictures and lines up books by height, swivel chairs are not for you. They will be perennially askew, never exactly as you arranged them. You also must forgo a drinks table between two swivel chairs, as the swivel*er* may knock it over.

Coffee Tables and Side Tables

You have some flexibility when it comes to the size of coffee tables and side tables. I prefer side tables that are the height of the sofa arm or slightly lower, but if they're a few inches taller, it isn't the end of the world. Side tables 24 inches high and lower can be difficult to find in a traditional style; contemporary occasional tables tend to be lower. As for width, if you intend to put a lamp on the table, the table should be at least 18 inches wide. Depth is of little concern, as long as the table isn't deeper than the sofa, which is highly unlikely.

A coffee table (or cocktail table[3]) can be wider than you think. If it's 18 to 24 inches narrower than your sofa, it will look appropriate. Coffee tables tend to be between 24 and 30 inches deep, which is fine most of the time. Ideally, they should be positioned 14 to 16 inches from the sofa.

As for height, if you plan to put your feet on your coffee table (which actually means it's a cocktail ottoman, because you would *never* put your feet on a table, correct?), it should be an inch or two lower than the sofa seat. The table can be taller if you plan to put out hors d'oeuvres on a regular basis.

Round coffee tables are tricky. (Oval tables are not!) A round table can look terrific, but please know that not everyone in the seating area will be able to reach it. Round coffee tables work best in the crook of a sectional, but even then, you will need end tables to ensure that everyone's drink has a place to land.

---

[3] I used to think that cocktail tables were slightly taller than coffee tables, but manufacturers don't differentiate.

Arranging Your Living Room Furniture

I love it when a room clearly announces where the furniture needs to be. There is a long wall for the sofa; two matching end tables (and matching lamps) will flank it; comfortable chairs will sit next to each table, facing each other; and a coffee table will be at the center of the arrangement. Ideally, another wall will be large enough to accommodate a console table, and *really* ideally, two small stools will live under it to be pulled out for additional seating. There may or may not be another short wall for, say, a desk, an occasional chair, or a bookcase. That is an obvious furniture arrangement. It is how my living room is set up, actually—and believe me, I have explored alternatives.

Often, however, furniture placement is *not* obvious, or there is more than one possible scenario. The drivers of furniture placement are the focal point and the function of the room.

The focal point of a room is often a fireplace, a beautiful view, or a television. The furniture should be arranged to feature, not block, the thing that is the center of attention; the sofa should not have its back to the fireplace, for example. (The exception: a corner fireplace. It's the *worst* for furniture placement! Make sure it looks nice, with candles or a pretty screen at the firebox and art above the mantel, but some piece of furniture likely will have its back to it. There's simply no way around it.)

Let's say you have a rectangular room with a fireplace smack-dab in the middle of a long wall. Pretty! Depending on the depth of the room, here are a few furniture placement options.

✦ **In a huge room:** The sofa floats in the room facing the fireplace, and the other furniture is arranged around it to create a conversation area. There may be a console table or large desk behind the sofa. Alternatively, two sofas can be placed perpendicular to the fireplace, facing each other, with two lounge chairs across from the fireplace.

✦ **In a medium-size room:** The sofa is against the wall opposite the fireplace, and two lounge chairs are next to the fireplace, perpendicular to it, facing each other. The path for walking is between the sofa and chairs, so the coffee table must be narrow or nonexistent.

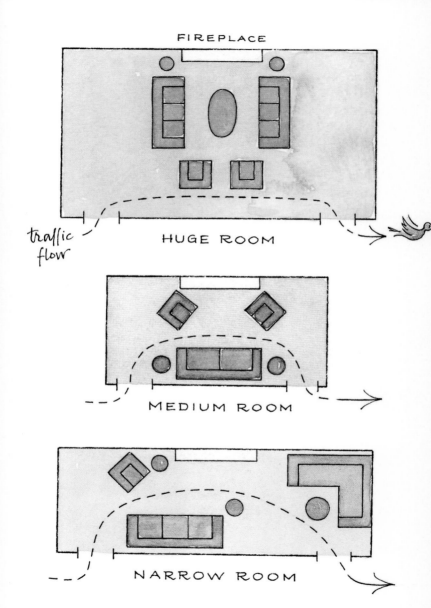

FIREPLACE

traffic flow

HUGE ROOM

MEDIUM ROOM

NARROW ROOM

✦ **In a narrow room:** Use the arrangement for
  a medium-size room (see opposite) or create
  two separate seating areas on either side of the
  fireplace. I once built a corner banquette on one
  side of the fireplace (and placed a game table in
  the crook), and on the other side, we created a
  small seating area with a slender sofa and chairs.
  It works beautifully.

Taking the function of the room into consideration, if you plan to use the room primarily for visiting
with guests, place the sofa where it makes sense and
make sure the other pieces are close enough to make
chatting, nibbling, and drinking easy. If the primary
function of the room is to watch television, the screen
is the focal point and furniture must be placed so that
everyone can see it.

What to Do About the TV

In response to the question of whether a television
may be mounted over a fireplace, I heave a big sigh.
Though the practice is widely accepted, I'd rather
you didn't. For one thing, a screen over a fireplace is

usually too high for comfortable viewing. Ideally, the TV will be in your line of sight when you are seated. For another, the screen will dominate the room. What about screens that look like mirrors or artwork, you ask? That is indeed better than a big black hole, but few people will be fooled. I will always prefer that you hang *real* art or a *real* mirror over the fireplace instead of a television. Here are some alternative placement options for the TV.

+ **On built-in shelving flanking the fireplace:** Picture a whole wall of built-ins (leaving a little breathing room on either side of the mantel) with deep cabinets on the bottom and shallow shelves on top that go all the way up to the ceiling. The TV can sit on the cabinet part, exposed, in front of the open shelves. It would be at eye level when you are seated across the room.

+ **On a low, freestanding cabinet next to the fireplace:** The cabinet should be a lovely piece of furniture, not a particleboard and metal "media stand" or, heaven forbid, a "TV armoire." These armoires are hulking, massive pieces of furniture

that dominate a room. (Pro tip: Search "dining room furniture" and look for cabinets and buffets. Watch the height, though: 30 inches is as tall as you should go.) Then put something on the other side of the fireplace for balance, such as a bookcase, an airy étagère,[4] a pretty desk, or a bench with art over it.

✦ **In another room—one without a fireplace:** I recommend placing the TV opposite the sofa on a low bookcase or the type of cabinet described above. I would be thrilled, however, if the TV were not the first thing I see when I walk into your lovely room. Try to place it on the same wall as the doorway instead.

---

[4] A freestanding shelving unit with no back or sides, usually for displaying objects rather than books. If you *do* choose to place books on a shelf or two, you will need attractive bookends to hold them upright.

DINING ROOM FURNITURE

Dining tables measure between 28 and 31 inches high. If you have an antique table, it's likely on the low end of that range. The height of a dining table is important, but the height of the apron—the vertical piece of wood under the table that connects the tabletop to the legs—is even more important. Your legs must fit comfortably under the table, but you also shouldn't feel like you need a booster seat. You should strive for at least 6 inches between the dining chair seat and the bottom of the apron. If you have dining chairs with arms, you must make sure *they* can fit under the table, too. (Guess who got so excited about a vintage dining table she found online that she neglected to measure her host chairs' arm height? A short, nearly invisible riser under each table leg did the trick, but how embarrassing!)

The seat height of dining chairs ranges from 17 to 20 inches, with 18 inches being common. Every inch makes a difference, so you really do need to ensure that you have the right chairs for your particular table.

Dining chairs with an overall height (from the floor to the top of the back) of 32 to 34 inches are appropriate for most rooms. Do not go taller on the chairs if your dining room is modest in size. If space is at a premium or if your taste is quite contemporary, keep chairs low—around 30 inches tall, the height of the table. If you have a gigantic room with a large dining table (let's say it's a minimum of 42 inches wide and 96 inches long), then tall chairs, say 40 or 42 inches high, will work. Anything taller than that is a statement, so proceed carefully.

The width of dining chairs tends to be more important than overall height. (The width of a chair doesn't necessarily determine comfort, by the way. Wider is rarely better.) Dining chairs 20 inches wide or narrower are the hardest to find, but they're worth the hunt. If you have space for chairs that are 22 inches wide, fantastic. Once you go wider than 24 inches, though, you officially have large dining chairs and should have a correspondingly large dining room.

As for how much space to leave between chairs, aim for 10 to 12 inches, with 6 inches as the minimum. If you find yourself with dining chairs that touch, consider making your dinner party buffet style. You can move a few dining chairs into the living area and bring small tables in from other rooms to ensure that everyone has a place to put their plate and drink.

BEDROOM FURNITURE

The days of the "bedroom suite," in which the bed, bedside tables, and dressers match, are long gone, thankfully. What an unimaginative way to decorate a room! It is much more appealing to mix things up a bit.

First, let's talk about placing light- and dark-stained wood furniture in the same room, which many people are loath to do. Let me assure you that it is perfectly fine! After all, we don't always consider the color of our hardwood floors when purchasing furniture, do we? Some people advise matching the *tone* of woods ("cool" or "warm"), but I find it easier to think about light and dark. You can put a mahogany bed in a room filled with light furniture, but try to repeat the dark wood elsewhere in the room, even in a small way. A stained wood picture frame, a tiny walnut drinks table, and/or a dark brown basket on the floor would be enough to make the mahogany bed look intentional.

Painted furniture is terrific with all stained wood. A navy blue bed is fun with a walnut dresser, and a white writing desk is so pretty with a pine headboard. Proceed carefully with painting furniture a bright color, as the effect can be childlike. Context is everything, though: A dark red headboard in a bedroom that is otherwise black and white would be quite sophisticated.

In addition to mixing different kinds of wood in your bedroom, consider adding a different material altogether. A small piece of furniture made with caning (a rocking chair!), bamboo (a console table!), pencil rattan (a headboard!), or wicker (a dressing table!) makes for an infinitely more interesting room than one filled exclusively with wooden furniture, even if the wood is of varying shades and colors.

Headboards

Headboards can be stained or painted wood (or another hard material), but upholstered headboards are undoubtedly my favorite. They bring a wonderful softness to a bedroom and balance hard-edged case goods. And talk about a terrific opportunity for color and pattern! Headboards come in many tasteful

square

corner-cut

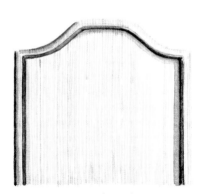

camelback

custom contour

shapes; my favorites are square, corner-cut, camelback, and custom contours. Regardless of the size of your room, I urge you to go with the tallest available. When I design a custom headboard, I may leave only 24 inches or so between the top of the headboard and the crown moulding. Counterintuitively, tall headboards make the ceiling feel higher, and they show off whatever gorgeous fabric you've chosen. (Plus, short headboards are often obscured by pillows.)

Headboards must be mounted on the wall or attached to a metal bed frame. In the latter case, a box spring is required to support the mattress. (I discuss box springs in more detail on the next page.) Then you place a bed skirt between the box spring and the mattress and let it fall neatly to the floor. A tailored (flat) bed skirt is tidy and sophisticated, and a ruched bed skirt, known in days of yore as a "dust ruffle," is informal and pretty.

Complete Beds

When people say "bed," they often mean a *complete* bed: a headboard attached to a frame in the same material—wood or fabric, for example—with or without a footboard. (Footboards are tricky, by the way. They eat up space in a small room, and they prevent you from perching on the end of the bed to put on your shoes. They also get in the way when you're trying to make the bed. Of course, if you already have a beautiful sleigh bed with a headboard and footboard, rejoice, because they are *gorgeous*.)

I must confess that I have never been a fan of metal beds. Modern ones look cold and sharp to me, even if they're painted a festive color. Antique iron bed frames have their place, but they do not mix well with contemporary furniture. They work best with a handmade quilt in a country setting; piled with pillows for a layered, bohemian look; or near a mahogany dresser in a traditional bedroom. They need *things* around them. Nothing screams "Victorian orphanage" more loudly than an antique iron bed in an underdecorated room, especially if that room is painted gray. Something to keep in mind.

Box Springs

All beds—metal-framed, upholstered, wooden—used to require a box spring under the mattress to provide structure and support. Today, though, box springs are disappearing as wooden-slatted beds gain popularity. To determine whether a bed requires a box spring, you must examine where the slats are placed within the bed frame. If the slats are near the top, the bed is a platform and does not need a box spring; if the slats are near the bottom, a box spring is required. (The box spring will be hidden within the bed frame, and the mattress will sit on top.) Some people put a mattress where a box spring should go, nestled inside the bed frame, but this is a mistake; it renders the bed difficult to make, and there often is an unattractive gap between the mattress and the bottom of the headboard.

Mattresses

Mattresses have become almost as confusing as light bulbs, in my opinion. When it comes to the *kind* of mattress you need—pillow-top, memory foam, soft, firm—you simply must visit mattress stores and test them. I'm sorry; there's just no other way.

As far as bed sizes are concerned, most people already know what they prefer (and what their room will accommodate). Please note that the sizes below are for mattresses only. If you're trying to determine whether a bed will fit between two windows, add 6 to 8 inches to account for the bed itself.

CALIFORNIA KING (72 by 84 inches)

I wouldn't worry too much about California kings, but in case you're interested, they're narrower and longer than regular kings. If you're a professional basketball player, a California king is essential.

KING (76 by 80 inches)

A king-size bed is the most comfortable if you sleep with a partner *and* a large dog. A queen really won't do.

QUEEN (60 by 80 inches)

If you are choosing between a queen and a full (double) bed for a guest bedroom (or for a child's room that may *become* a guest bedroom someday), go for the queen. Almost no one puts two adults in a full anymore.

FULL/DOUBLE (54 by 74 inches)

If a bedroom belongs to a single adult, a full bed is fine. It's certainly preferable to a twin. If there's even the smallest chance that said adult may acquire a bedmate, however (and if the room is large enough), please see above. The extra acreage that a queen bed provides is nice for two people.

TWIN (38 by 75 inches)

Twin beds are another excellent option for guest bedrooms. A single adult will be perfectly comfortable for a brief stay, and I love the look of a pair of twin beds with matching headboards. There's something so tidy about it. It's worth noting that two twin mattresses pushed together *almost* equal a king. The width is the same, but the length will be a bit shorter. Nonetheless, pushing two twin beds together and using king sheets is an option if you are hosting a couple who cannot bear to be apart overnight.

TWIN XL (38 by 80 inches)

I can barely stand to dignify "twin XL" beds with a mention, but I suppose I must. They are *so* obnoxious. As you undoubtedly know, they are found only at summer camps and in college dorms, and I find it supremely annoying that I have to buy special sheets for them.

The only thing worth knowing about twin XL beds is that two of them pushed together create a king.

Bedside Tables and Dressers

I like bedside tables to be approximately the same height as the top of your mattress. This is a comfortable height for reaching a glass of water, putting down your book, and turning off the bedside lamp.

Practicality tends to drive the selection of dressers. If you have a long wall in your bedroom, a low, wide dresser is terrific, because the surface can hold many objects, both functional (a bowl for change, a jewelry box) and decorative (a framed picture of your cat). If you don't have space for a wide dresser, a tall, skinny one is just fine.

ANTIQUES

The term "antique" is applied to furniture that is a hundred years old or older. "Vintage" is less well defined. Some people say it describes items older than twenty-five years; others say fifty years. I was in a consignment shop not too long ago, and the perky young woman behind the counter exclaimed proudly, "These earrings are vintage! They're from the eighties!" As a person who had owned the same earrings as a teenager,

I did not appreciate the sales pitch, technically accurate though it may have been.

Antiques-packed rooms are generally out of fashion right now, which is tragic. But using antiques selectively can create a wonderfully layered design. Here are some tips for using antiques to create a beautiful room that also feels current.

✦ **Don't allow too many in one room:** Two is generally enough.

✦ **Mix materials:** Placing antiques alongside modern pieces creates a lovely, relaxed, personalized space. If you have a giant mahogany console table in your living room, consider bringing in a bamboo étagère, a Lucite waterfall coffee table, or marble-topped side tables for contrast.

✦ **Don't pair antiques with old-fashioned lamps:** Fussy lamps (such as cloisonné or porcelain) are the fastest way to make a room feel stodgy.

✦ **Add something lighthearted:** This will counteract the heaviness of the antiques. For

example, wallpaper with a light background, modern fabrics, or a needlepoint pillow shaped like a dachshund. (I made that last one up, and now I want it.)

If you don't care to live with many antiques or pay for storage, I give you permission to get rid of them, family pieces or not. While we're at it, I also give you permission to part with rugs and artwork you hate. You must love your home. I insist upon it. And that's going to be difficult if you have cringeworthy (to you) items lurking about. (But if you have a houseful of antiques and you love them, you've just become my Person of the Day!)

FURNITURE STYLES

You will notice, Gentle Reader, that I have avoided any discussion of style in this chapter: nary a mention of Victorian, art deco, mid-century, or contemporary. This is because I believe that original, interesting interior design results from the *mixing* of styles (and eras, colors, and patterns), so I will never advise you to choose one style over another.

That said, I must address the term "transitional." It is used to describe individual pieces of furniture ("a transitional-style sofa") as well as an overall aesthetic ("my style is transitional"). But what does "transitional" mean? *Nothing,* that's what. A cross between traditional and contemporary? Appealing to people who are unsure about what they like but want their homes to look noncommittally modern according to today's standards? No. You're better than that. Here are some words you may use instead: *current, fresh, clean-lined.* There's no need to use the word "transitional" ever again.

4

LIGHTING

Nothing beats
a table lamp

The importance of lighting cannot be overemphasized. Not only does every room require the option of either dim or bright lighting depending on how the room is being used at any given time, but the *quality* of light is critical. As is the placement of light fixtures, both hardwired and freestanding. I am not being dramatic: Many a dinner party has been seriously compromised by baseball stadium–level lighting, whether from a chandelier, table lamps, or both.

OVERHEAD LIGHTING

Many people assume that every room requires over-head lighting. Not so! A central chandelier (see page 80) can look fantastic in a dining room—or a living room or bedroom—but it cannot provide all of your light. Ditto for a flush mount or semi–flush mount ceiling fixture. (Unless it is in a front hall and *must* provide all the light for that area. If that's the case, please pay close attention to the section about light bulbs on page 88.)

With regard to recessed lights, if you already have them, fine. If you do not, please think twice before installing them. I generally am opposed to punching unnecessary holes in the ceiling, especially if your house is from the 1920s or earlier. The holes are not invisible, and too many can draw attention away from the beautifully decorated room below. (A small spot-light trained on artwork is the exception.)

It should go without saying that *all* of your over-head lights, surface-mounted or recessed, should be on dimmers. You simply don't know from one moment to the next what light level you will need: Is it a cloudy morning or a bright afternoon? Is it a summertime cocktail hour or a wintertime Scrabble marathon in front of the fire? I'm often criticized by my husband for surreptitiously lowering a room's light level, whether I'm in my own house or not. Sepulchral darkness is my preferred setting. When my children complain that they can't see their dinner, I point out that we have perfectly good candles to guide us.

CHANDELIERS

If you promise to supplement it with floor and table lamps, a chandelier can be a lovely addition to a room. In living rooms, family rooms, and bedrooms, please allow *at least* 7½ feet between the floor and the bottom of the fixture so your tallest guests may walk freely beneath it.

In a dining room, I like the bottom of a chandelier to be about 33 inches from the surface of a dining table, although many designers say that 30 inches is enough. This is a rule I break all the time, though. Hang your chandelier higher if it is unusually large or if it can't be centered directly over the dining table

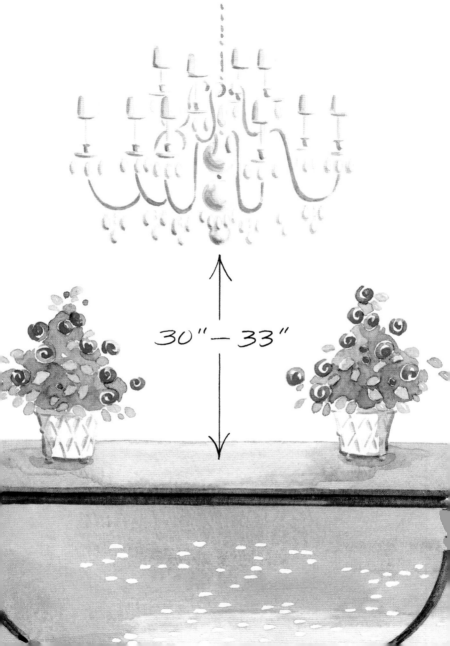

30"–33"

(bringing it up de-emphasizes the off-kilter-ness). As far as diameter is concerned, room size is more important than table size. A chandelier less than 18 inches in diameter is small and requires a correspondingly modest-size room. It may work over a kitchen table, but it probably will not be large enough for your dining room. A 24- to 30-inch diameter is appropriate for a normal-size dining room, and anything greater than that is *very* large—think twice.

TABLE LAMPS

Table and floor lamps—particularly those with three-way sockets so you can adjust the brightness—are preferable to overhead lighting. They're more flexible from a decorating standpoint, they can provide either ambient or task lighting, and the light they cast (from the side) is more flattering than light from above. (Overhead light casts shadows, which is why bathroom sconces should be on either side of your mirror whenever possible.)

In addition to being superior to overhead lighting, table lamps are decorative objects, and as such are a great opportunity for sparkle, shine, and color. Lamps with a metal finish, such as brass or nickel, are extremely versatile, as are nonmetal but metal-*looking* finishes such as antique mirror or mercury glass. Heavy crystal lamps brighten up a space even when they're not turned on, and they're always tasteful, always appropriate. (Please do not place crystal lamps in direct sunlight, however; it's a fire hazard. Ask me how I know this.) Colorful ceramic lamps also can be fun if the design calls for them.

As with rugs, don't go too small on your table lamps. The larger the room, the larger the lamp. A client swore up and down that a 34-inch-tall lamp was going to be *way* too large for his family room. But guess what? The room was airy, the side tables were substantial, and the lamps (yes, I sneaked in a pair) were perfect. He agreed in the end. Here are some general guidelines.

+ 27 to 30 inches from base to top of lampshade is probably the right height for side tables in your living room or family room; taller if the room is unusually large. The lamps will look big at first, especially if you had nothing there previously.

But give it a bit of time, and you'll see that they're scaled appropriately.

✦ 24 inches is also a good height for many situations—on bedside tables, desks, or side tables in smallish rooms with ceilings around 8 feet tall.

✦ The term "accent lamp" refers to a much smaller, often whimsical lamp—a 15-inch porcelain rabbit, for example. Accent lamps are darling on a secretary, a tiny foyer table, or even an étagère if they fit.

FLOOR LAMPS

In addition to providing a lot of light, floor lamps can add a wonderful, even sculptural, presence to a room. Please make sure they're not hanging out all alone in a corner, though; floor lamps look best when they're next to something else.

When it comes to size, 60 to 72 inches is a good standard height *if the lamp is not next to a sofa or chair.* Next to an étagère, a cabinet, or a bookcase, a lamp this height is usually perfect. Lamps taller than 72 inches are best in large rooms with high ceilings, say 9 to 12 feet.

When a lamp is positioned right next to a sofa or chair, protect your eyeballs by making sure the shade is roughly in line with your head when you're seated. Usually, 48 to 54 inches tall is ideal. Reading lamps can be much shorter, with metal shades lower than your eyes so that light shines directly onto your book or newspaper.

As an aside, I hate torchières of any height. Those are the floor lamps (often stained glass) that direct light up toward the ceiling. They don't light what you need lit, such as people and surfaces, and the light they cast can make a room feel lonely. If you already have one, please replace it. Or at least supplement the light with well-placed table lamps so your room has a cozy glow.

LAMPSHADES

Shapes

The most common lampshade shapes are "empire," which is gently cone-shaped, and "drum," which is like a fat tube—the sides go straight up and down. There's no difference in function; the choice is entirely a matter of taste. You can't go wrong with empire shades—they are timeless and lovely. Drum shades are more modern-looking (they gained popularity in the late 1950s and '60s) and fairly innocuous. There are many other types of lampshades, of course—bell (in which the sides swoop between a small top and wider bottom), rectangular, cut corner (rectangular with the corners lopped off), and pagoda (a fancy cut-corner style)—but if you stick with empire and drum shades, they'll look terrific in any design context.

Materials

As far as lampshade material is concerned, I prefer linen or silk. A fabric shade looks intentional, as though you chose it for that specific lamp. That said, paper lampshades are totally acceptable in casual living spaces and children's bedrooms. If you're dead serious about making a room look coordinated, consider a patterned fabric lampshade. Envision a cornflower-blue gingham lampshade that matches the Peter Rabbit curtains in a nursery. Perfection!

Please keep in mind that lampshades that are not translucent (e.g., a metal shade, or a tasteful black shade with a gold foil lining) will direct light up and down but not sideways. That doesn't mean you shouldn't have one or two; it just means you can't depend on them alone to light a room.

Sizing

Lampshade measurements are indicated by three numbers. They are, in order, the top diameter, the bottom diameter, and the length of the slant. (At least, this is the order in which lampshade measurements are listed in the United States.) I find the slant part terribly confusing, to be honest.

If you need to replace a lampshade, rather than bringing the shade dimensions (or even the shade) to the shop, I strongly recommend taking the lamp itself. It's inconvenient, but it's the best way to ensure a proper match. Quality lampshades are not inexpensive, so you want to get them right.

Fittings

A fitting is the metal part that attaches a shade to a lamp. There are a few different styles—clip, spider, and uno—but a spider fitting is the most common type in the U.S. It is a metal X at the top of the shade with a hole in the center; you place it on top of the harp (the frame that goes from the lamp base around and above the bulb) and screw it in place with a finial. Clip shades are used on chandeliers and on other small lamps.

LIGHT BULBS

Light bulbs have never been more confusing. All I want is an energy-efficient, long-lasting bulb that emits a soft, flattering light. Is that so much to ask? The answer, it would seem, is yes.

For years, the four most common types of bulbs have been incandescent, halogen, CFL (compact fluorescent), and LED (light-emitting diode). Incandescent bulbs are what we think of when we think of a light bulb. The light they cast can be flattering, but incandescent bulbs are inefficient and last only about a year. Halogens are somewhat energy-efficient, but they can become dangerously hot. Thankfully, you may now forget about incandescent and halogen bulbs because they are no longer produced. You also may ignore CFL bulbs. They, too, are being phased out in many places, but even if they weren't, I would forbid you to buy them. Efficiency is the *only* thing CFLs have going for them. They're ugly (picture a squashed tubular coil), they take a while to achieve maximum brightness after you turn them on, the light they emit is cold and harsh, and as a bonus, they contain mercury and require special disposal methods. No, thank you.

That leaves us with LED bulbs. Originally prohibitively expensive, LEDs have come down dramatically in price since they first hit the market. LEDs have many excellent qualities. They're remarkably energy-efficient, and they have a lifespan of nine to twenty years—or even more. The complaint about LEDs used to be that the light was extremely bright

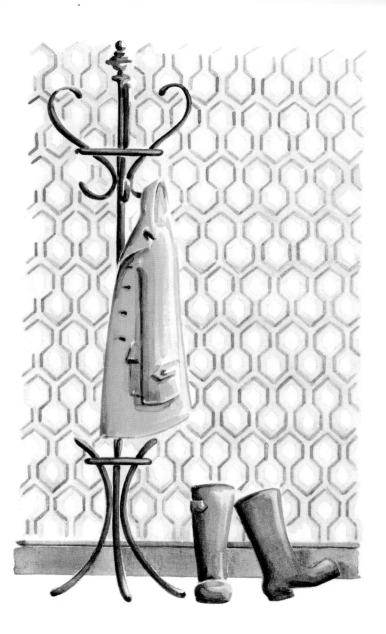

5

PAINT & WALLPAPER

Who decided that "sophisticated"
must equal "gray"?

When it comes to walls, Gentle Reader, what opportunities await you! The right paint or wallpaper will complement your rugs and furniture, provide a dynamic backdrop for your artwork, and, of course, create a mood. It is no exaggeration to say that what you put on your walls sets the aesthetic and visceral tone for your entire home.

You likely are comfortable enough with the *idea* of painting your walls, although selecting a color may be daunting. Select you must, however, so I hope the following information will be helpful.

PAINT COLORS

I don't know how it happened, but somewhere along the way, interior designers and then the decorating public decided that the only way to make a room feel elegant was to paint it gray. Not true. Color can be elegant. *Bold* color can be elegant.

Did this happen because gray is a Realtor favorite, and many people don't repaint when they move into a new house? Realtors say that it's easier for prospective buyers to picture themselves in a home that's been neutralized to gray. I can appreciate that (in theory, at least). But if you're currently living with gray on gray on gray, may I gently remind you that paint is the least expensive, fastest way to update a room, and that you should paint every seven to ten years anyway? If you paint at least one room a color that isn't gray, I promise that you will not regret it.

Before selecting paint colors, you must take into consideration your light conditions, other hues[1] in the

---

[1] For extra credit: "Hue" is the purest form of color—the colors on the color wheel. Hues are intense. A "tone" is a color with gray added. Tones are less saturated than hues.

room, the color palette in the rest of your house, and, of course, your personality. You should live with the colors you love, even if you have to tone them down for decorating purposes. If you adore blue, for example, I'm going to propose some super-light blues and some super-dark ones.

If you were hoping to find specific paint number and manufacturer recommendations here, I must disappoint you. I believe a broader discussion of color will be more helpful to you. Here are my thoughts, starting with the ever-popular blue and working our way around the color wheel.

Blue

Pale blue is indisputably lovely everywhere. It's always a good option for bedrooms and bathrooms (blue makes dingy white tile look brighter), but recently I've found myself encouraging clients to consider an extremely light blue for living rooms, too. It's a fresh, unexpected choice, don't you think? Aqua, a warm blue, has been the preferred version of light blue in recent years. It's cheerful and accessible. Cool blues are coming back, though, and they feel more reserved and formal to me.

Dark blue is so versatile, it's crazy. It's a dignified choice for libraries and dining rooms, and I recently painted a primary bedroom dark blue. It was, in a word, dreamy. We did drapes in a similar color; the room was an odd shape, and using the same color everywhere had a unifying effect.

Green

A tricky color, green. More than any other color, greens are strongly associated with certain time periods: 1950s mint, '70s avocado, the Kelly green of the '80s, sage in the '90s . . . see what I mean? That said, dark olive green (with its yellow undertone) and bottle green (which has a blue undertone) are some of the most elegant colors around. They're so rich, and they look beautiful with almost any color you can think of. I painted a little boy's bedroom walls light aqua and did the trim olive green, and it was fabulous. Put olive and dark orange together, and you have a terrific combination for a family room or study. Bottle green is so English to me. I especially love it in dining rooms, because I think it looks gorgeous with dark wood furniture.

I also like a soft fern green for bedrooms (including my own!), grassy greens in children's rooms, and incredibly dark, dusty greens in libraries. Light, fresh greens are a favorite for kitchen walls . . . although a contractor once told me that he would *never* paint a kitchen green because it reminds him of mold. I think more of lettuce, but to each their own.

Yellow

Yellow is one of my favorite colors, but it can be a tough sell in decorating. When I *have* gotten clients to agree to it, it's been an extremely light hue. I've used crisp yellows in hallways and bedrooms and creamy yellows in living rooms. Yellow is a cheerful, uplifting color, and once you get the right hue (not too orange, not too green), it can be lovely.

Orange and Red

Despite the popularity of red dining rooms in the late aughts and early teens, red and orange can be difficult to use on walls, especially in their "screaming" versions (e.g., midlife-crisis-Porsche and tangerine). But in their deepest iterations, red and orange can

be wonderfully comforting. Imagine an enclosed TV room the color of the Hermès logo, or a bedroom (yes, I said bedroom!) in a red so deep it's nearly brown. Sumptuous.

Pink

While it is not technically on the color wheel, I feel I must include some comments about pink. Light pink—"blush," in today's parlance—has become quite popular. My north-facing living room is blush right now, and I love it! And a dear friend is painting her kitchen walls super-light pink *as I type*! Because light pink is universally flattering, it's a natural choice for guest bedrooms and bathrooms. I'd also love to see more hallways and living rooms in light pink. You really can treat it as a neutral.

Purple

Lavender is a terrific bedroom color. I'm about to install lavender-and-white wallpaper in a bedroom with a cherry-red antique rug. It sounds nuts, but it's going to be amazing. At the other end of the light/dark scale, I've also become a fan of aubergine, preferably in a dry, chalky finish. It's rich and cozy, especially when paired with dark green . . . perfect for a dining room, a den, or a guest bedroom with a fireplace. As for the mid-tone purple most commonly found on cartoon dinosaurs: No. Just no.

White

"We'll just paint the walls white" is the silliest thing a person can say. If you've ever been in a paint store, you know that there are literally *thousands* of whites. Each has a warm or cool undertone—there's really no such thing as a "neutral" white. In addition, each white tends to have the teensiest drop of another color in it. Some grayish whites veer blue, for example, and some creamy whites approach yellow.

Whites change dramatically depending on the direction a room faces (or how many exposures a room has), light conditions, and large items nearby. A white-walled room with a royal blue rug will look different from the same room with a yellow rug. You must, *must* paint several posterboards the shades of white you are considering and tape them to the walls. Look at them at different times of day over several days, and move them around. This little exercise will help you home in on the *right* white for your space.

And a note on pairing white with black: It's a classic combo—and I love nothing more than a black-and-white checkerboard floor—but it's overrated in decorating. A room that is entirely black and white is boring and cold. And, dare I say, unimaginative. It looks smashing, though, when you introduce one other color—*any* color. Black and white with grassy green? Fresh and amazing. With dark beige? Extraordinarily sophisticated. With yellow? Buzzy and vaguely historic. You catch my drift.

Gray

Lest you think that I have it in for gray, let me assure you that I do not. It can be very pretty, especially light gray with ivory (*not* bright white) trim, or in its darkest, charcoal-y-est forms. I simply object to its being thought of as the *only* option if you wish to create a serene, elegant space.

PAINT COLORS ON TRIM

When walls are dark, you must go darker on the trim. The effect can be unpleasantly jarring when the contrast between wall and trim is too great. Additionally, I'm sorry to say, a dark-walled room with bright white trim can look cheap. (Of course, navy with bright white is quite nautical, so if that's the desired effect, please proceed.) Don't worry: Your eye won't register the difference if you walk through, say, an ivory living room with off-white trim to a dark blue dining room with beige trim.

Another option for trim, of course, is to paint it the same color as the walls. It's a terribly sophisticated look. Furthermore, repeating the wall color on trim has the advantage of enlarging a small room and smoothing out a room with multiple windows and doors—when there's practically more trim than wall. Be sure to use an appropriate finish for trim: satin, semi-gloss, or high-gloss (more on this to come).

PAINT FINISHES

Flat

Flat paint has no sheen, so it's best for imperfect walls (such as those in historic houses) because it de-emphasizes bumps and ridges. Be warned, however, that walls in a flat finish are difficult to clean. Scrubbing a smudge can result in an unattractive shiny spot if you're not careful.

Eggshell

An eggshell finish, which has the tiniest bit of sheen, is easier to wipe down than flat paint, and it gives you a bit of a glow, which is nice. It highlights imperfections ever so slightly, though, so it's best on new, smooth walls. I always use an eggshell finish in kitchens and bathrooms, regardless of the home's age, because it's more resistant to moisture than flat.

Satin

Located on the sheen scale somewhere between eggshell and semi-gloss, a satin finish is, well, semi-flat. I've started using a satin finish on trim when a client's style skews modern. Satin paint applied by a professional with a sprayer (for a "shop finish") is also ideal on cabinetry. Some people like to use satin paint on kitchen and bath walls, but that makes me nervous because of the sheen . . . please read on.

Semi-Gloss and High-Gloss

Unless they are painstakingly lacquered,[2] shiny walls are gross. Particularly disgusting is semi-gloss paint that has been applied to walls with a roller, thus producing an unattractive orange-peel effect. It looks tacky and thoughtless and makes me quite angry, to be honest. Semi-gloss paint *is* terrific, however, for most trim. I love high-gloss paint on trim also, especially in older houses. You do see the brushstrokes if you're hand-painting with a semi- or high-gloss finish paint, but I find that charming. For a supersmooth look, the paint must be applied with a sprayer (by a professional), which is labor-intensive but yields beautiful results.

[2] Lacquer is a treatment involving layers and layers of professionally applied high-gloss paint with meticulous sanding between each coat. The result is a glassy, perfectly smooth, shiny finish. It's refined and dramatic all at once . . . truly swoon-worthy.

strié

tone-on-tone

two-tone geometric

scenic

WALLPAPER

When I say "wallpaper," are you immediately hit with the memory of large-scale, multicolor floral patterns in the guest bedroom of your grandmother's house? Is that why you shut down emotionally and turn off your listening ears when I mention it? Wallpaper doesn't have to be old-fashioned! And if you don't have much artwork, wallpaper should be your best friend: A large framed mirror on wallpaper can work wonders.

I happen to *love* bold, dramatic wallpaper—floral, scenic, abstract—but I recognize that it's not everyone's cup of tea. There are nonthreatening kinds of wallpaper, such as tone-on-tone (in neutrals, such as white on beige, or colors, such as light and dark blue). I'm secretly hopeful that the options below will serve as your gateway to adventurous decorating and that before you know it, you'll be plastering Schumacher's Chiang Mai dragons all over your dining room.

Two-Tone

Two-tone patterns are incredibly versatile. I once had a client agree to a simple blue-and-white wallpaper in her family room. I was thrilled, as family and living rooms seem to be the final frontier for patterned wallpaper. The effect is fresh, bright, and cheerful. We did the sofa in a light blue and two comfy chairs in a grassy green, and the client is so happy. She's a British landscape architect, and she says that the room has an English garden feel that she adores. You can't give me a bigger compliment, frankly.

Strié

Strié wallpaper—paper with a tiny stripe in two shades of a color—is another lovely option for a subtle wallcovering. It provides the color variation of grasscloth (see below) without the shine.

Grasscloth

I'm a huge fan of grasscloth, which is a wallcovering made of natural grasses (or, for my allergy-prone clients, vinyl that resembles grasscloth, which I swear can look terrific). Grasscloth has been around since the late 1950s and has gone in and out of fashion ever since. It's a wonderful material offering slight variations in color, so you don't have to worry that your blue chairs won't match your blue walls. They'll probably look great together. Grasscloth also has a natural sheen, which subtly reflects light in a most pleasing way.

TRIM COLORS WITH WALLPAPER

A delightful benefit of decorating with wallpaper is that a whole new world of trim colors opens up. Of course, you *can* use contrasting trim colors with painted walls—as in the little boy's room in olive and aqua I described earlier—but two different colors of paint in a room is a *statement*. When you wallpaper, it simply makes sense to pull out one of the colors in the pattern or match the field[3] to your trim. An absolutely gorgeous look I saw not so long ago: wallpaper with blue, light blue, and ivory flowers on a dark brown field, paired with dark brown trim. It was unexpected and oh-so-elegant.

As for trim finishes, the rules for painted rooms apply to those with wallpaper: Satin is great if your home skews modern; semi-gloss is universally appropriate; and high-gloss is excellent for traditional interiors.

[3] Background color.

6

ART

You cannot *do*
without it

And now for something else to put on your walls: art. It's magic! And it's essential. Nothing distinguishes your home like art. Nothing personalizes it quite as effectively. I do understand, however, that art can be intimidating in every way: the finding, the framing, and the hanging. Let's see if we can demystify things a bit.

ACQUIRING ART

Many of us have at least a few pieces of art we like. I don't care whether they're from a Madison Avenue gallery or a street fair. If you have it and you like it, you can find a great spot for it in your house. But chances are that you don't have *quite enough* art. And the art you have may be too small. Generally speaking, a house needs at least a few large pieces—say 20 by 30 inches or bigger.

It is a myth that all art is expensive. Original art—such as paintings, silkscreens, and engravings—and quality prints are available for a reasonable price in many places. The internet, for one: Etsy is a gift to the fledgling collector or home-furnisher, as are the social media accounts of creative people. Flea markets and vintage stores are another great source. (Don't be put off by tacky or ornate frames, by the way: Reframing works wonders on a tired piece of art. More about framing on page 115.) Print and map shops. Art schools, which have student exhibitions on a regular basis. Your home of origin when your parents downsize (more on inherited artwork below). Even galleries with budget-friendly items. They exist!

Some of my clients say they haven't bought art because they're waiting until they go on vacation or otherwise find themselves in a situation conducive to art acquisition. But you know what? Art can strike when we least expect it. Many years ago, my husband and I were in a restaurant that happened to be exhibiting the work of local artists. We were intrigued by a landscape painting in which the sky was acid yellow. It was fabulous. There was no price listed, but the artist's name was. When we found ourselves still talking about the painting days later, we decided we should act. A quick internet search put us in touch with the artist. The price was fair, so we drove to his studio with a check,[1] and when the restaurant decided to hang something different on its walls, we picked up the painting. It's been hung in several different places in our house, and we still love it. Did we expect to buy a painting after going out that night? No. But what a bonus—and a mildly interesting story, to boot.

[1] A quaint form of payment involving a piece of paper, a writing implement, and a hand.

A Word on Inherited Art

Remember our earlier discussion of antique furniture (page 71), and how you shouldn't have it if you don't like it? The same goes for paintings of (or formerly belonging to) relatives who are no longer with us. Art that has been "handed down," as it were. If you don't like something, please do not have it in your house. It's that simple.

FRAMING ART

The right frame can transform a mediocre piece of art into an attractive one that looks thoughtfully selected. You can breathe new life into a ho-hum painting previously trapped by a worm-eaten, rusty, or faux-gilded frame, and the "new" piece will add character to the dullest room.

"Ah," you may be saying. "But how do you know when you've found the 'right' frame?" That, Gentle Reader, is the trick. There are no hard-and-fast rules, I'm sorry to say. Simple "gallery frames" (medium width, no curves, no beveled edges) are a good place to start. They enhance many different styles of art, and their minimalist design is appropriate for traditional and contemporary interiors alike.

Select a frame that complements the *piece*, and don't worry too much about the context in which it will hang. For example, let's say you've fallen in love with a nineteenth-century English engraving of a bird, and your home is contemporary in style. I recommend that you use a traditional frame: perhaps a narrow, gold-painted frame with a bevel. As for where to hang the engraving in your sleek modern house: in a small nook by itself. It will not look its best next to your Rothko.

Please do not default to black picture frames. They are not neutral; they are a choice. Black frames look terrific with many styles of art, especially when the art has black *in* it. But framing a brown, ocher, and red landscape from your grandmother in black would be a mistake—especially if the frame is from a crafts or home goods store and you've kept the flimsy, bright white mat that came with it. No, no, no. Instead, natural wood, either light (such as maple) or dark (such as walnut), is incredibly versatile. There's a shade to complement every work of art.

I'm partial to wooden frames that are painted gold or silver. The profile can be clean and gallery-like or have detail, such as ridges or a bevel, but if you keep the width modest, a metallic-painted frame can brighten up a piece like nobody's business. (Please do not confuse "metallic" with "metal," which you are to avoid at all costs. If you grew up in the 1970s or '80s, you likely have a piece of art from your parents with a metal frame. I'm giving it to you straight: It looks dated, and you should replace it at your earliest opportunity.)

Some paintings don't need to be framed at all. Artists working on canvas sometimes continue an image onto the edges of a piece, indicating that the art may be hung just as it is. If the sides are *not* painted, or if you simply decide that you'd like the painting to look a little more finished, you may use a floater frame. That is a special, extra-deep frame that leaves a little space—usually less than an inch—between the painting and the frame. Glass is not used with floater frames, or on oil paintings in general, by the way, unless said paintings are in the Louvre and need protection from vandals.

One final tip: When you're hanging a piece in which the art extends to the very edges of the paper or canvas, consider adding a light-colored mat, especially if the picture will be hung on a dark wall. This will give you some separation between the art and the wall—a little breathing room, as it were. You'll be surprised at how much a picture will pop when it has some space around it. Please notice that I said a "light-colored," not "white," mat. If you use a stark white mat on a piece that isn't blinding white itself (i.e., anything more than a few years old), the artwork will look dirty and tired. Conversely, off-white, ivory, and beige mats will really perk up a vintage map or the still life your mother drew in college. Mats in linen or silk are particularly elegant.

WHERE TO HANG YOUR ART (AND MIRRORS, WHILE WE'RE AT IT)

Small wall, small art; large wall, large art. Right? Actually, yes. If you are looking for one tip and one tip only, that's it. Thank you, and good night.

But let's go a little further and talk about the two most challenging—and yet most common—places we hang art: over a sofa and over a fireplace. We have less flexibility over the fireplace. That spot requires one large piece, and that piece could be a mirror.

To digress for a moment, I have complicated feelings about mirrors. They can play very nicely with artwork, but some people buy mirrors *instead of* art, which is a grave error. Nothing says "I'm afraid of making a decorating mistake" more loudly than a room with one mirror per wall and no art. (Using mirrors intentionally is another story: Three identical mirrors marching in a line over the sofa, or several small mirrors integrated into a gallery wall, could be quite striking.)

Back to the fireplace: I recommend hanging one large piece (or a diptych or triptych, which reads as one piece) because an assortment of unlike pieces just looks messy here. The fireplace itself provides visual interest, so a single piece of art or a mirror—perhaps with a tall decorative object at either end of the mantel—gives you plenty to look at.

One large piece also looks terrific over a sofa, and as the sofa is often the first thing you see when you enter a living room, that artwork has pride of place. If the picture isn't *quite* large enough (say, less than half the sofa's width), make sure you're hanging it low, even as low as a foot above the sofa. Feel free to place two small matching items on either side of it, such as candle sconces. Alternatively, the wall over the sofa can handle a collection of artwork, unlike the wall over a fireplace. You're eye to eye with the art, so you can see details, and multiple pieces of art can fill a lot of wall. You also are able to manipulate your perception of a space with a gallery wall: Extend the art nearly up to the ceiling and the room looks taller; hang pieces along the entire width of the sofa and the room looks bigger overall. (For more on gallery walls, see page 124.)

While it's fairly obvious that the areas above the sofa and the fireplace require artwork, I also love hanging art in unexpected places. I've seen pieces successfully positioned on an (untiled) kitchen backsplash, above a door frame, and on a closet door. My fireplace has a bizarrely tall (around 18-inch) expanse of wood between the firebox and the mantel, so I hung a tiny painting there. It looks great, if I do say so myself. Rather, it looks *normal*; when it was just a big empty spot, it looked odd.

As an important aside, a room's color palette need not dictate which pieces of art you hang in it. It's lovely when the colors of a painting work in a particular room, but by "work," I don't mean "match." I just mean "look great in." I once hung a client's large orange-and-green abstract painting over a contemporary purple sofa, and it was quite striking.

That example notwithstanding, please don't grow too attached to certain pieces of art in certain spots, because you should move your art around from time to time. (Nail holes are usually covered by the newly placed pieces, but if not, a smidge of spackle and a Q-tip's worth of leftover paint—which you should keep in a mason jar, by the way—will mask the offending mark.) We become so used to our surroundings that we don't *see* things anymore. When you rearrange your art, everything looks fresh and new. One of my clients is an amazingly talented collector. No sooner do we finish hanging his latest acquisitions than he brings new pieces into the mix. He and I just keep shuffling things around, and as a result, the house looks different every time I go there. See? Magic.

HOW TO HANG YOUR ART

If you have the means, you will save yourself time, heartache, and holes in your walls by hiring professional art installers. It's not as expensive as you'd think, they're speedy, and they double-hang[2] so the pictures won't get crooked if they're nudged by a shoulder or an aggressive feather duster. Art installers don't guide you on placement, though. You must use your own judgment for that.

Even those of us who are, shall we say, *vertically challenged* tend to hang artwork too high. In general, the center of a picture should be approximately 5 feet from the floor. If you're hanging several pictures horizontally, line up the centers of the pictures rather than the tops or bottoms of the frames.

Artwork shouldn't look like it's floating in space; it must relate to the object below it, be that a sofa, mantel, or table. I mentioned on page 119 that you should hang a painting fairly close to the top of a sofa, especially if the painting is slightly too small for the wall.

---

[2] Screw two D-rings onto the back of each piece.

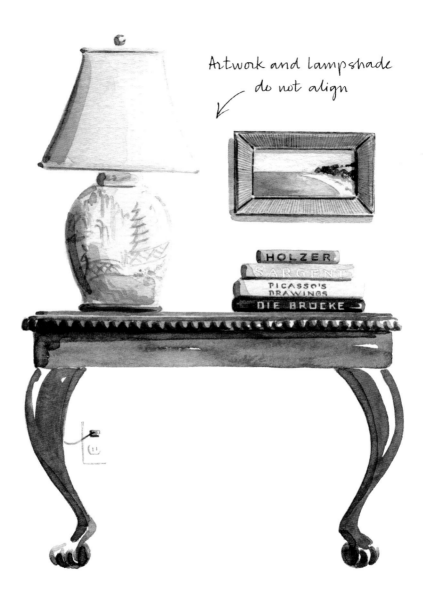

Artwork and lampshade
do not align

The low position connects the art to the furniture and de-emphasizes the painting's modest scale. The whole arrangement then feels intentional.

Here's another example. It's a bit complex, but stay with me. Let's say you have an end table (round or rectangular; it doesn't matter), a lamp, and a small-ish painting. Place the lamp off-center on the table, and hang the picture next to it, *very low*. If you have nothing else on the table (which you should, but we'll address that in the next chapter), the bottom of the painting might be only 6 or 8 inches from the table-top. If you have some tall objects on the table, the painting may be hung a bit higher, but it's also okay if the objects overlap the picture a bit. Just make sure the top of the frame is either above or below the top of the lampshade, not in line with it.

GALLERY WALLS

At last. The gallery wall. Also called an "art wall," a gallery wall is a collection of varied pieces of art-work or photographs hung close together in a visu-ally pleasing arrangement. As with selecting the right frames (see page 115), when it comes to creating these arrangements, there are no fixed rules, although you will have an easier time hanging an odd number of pieces than an even one, unless you're hanging them in a grid.

As random and effortless as you would like your gallery wall to look, it helps to have a common thread among the pieces. Perhaps it's the subject: They're all portraits, or landscapes, or pictures of flowers. Perhaps it's the medium: They're all oil paintings or artsy photographs or pencil sketches. Perhaps they're all black-and-white, or—although this is harder to carry off, as it can look juvenile—they're predominantly the same color.

With regard to the sizes of the pieces on the wall, it's perfectly fine to mix them up. I do recommend a *range* of sizes, though; it can look strange to have one very large item (poster size, let's say) among many tiny (postcard-size) items. If one piece is considerably larger than the others, do not put it in the middle of the arrangement unless you want the focus to be on that item rather than on the gallery wall as a whole. Rather, if you think of the wall in columns, place a large piece on the left, small things in the center (think of them as one unit), and two large-to-medium pieces stacked on the right (think of *them* as one unit). It's difficult to explain, I know, and if you search for "how to hang a gallery wall" online, you will find a range of tips, many of them useful. Because the arrangement of a gallery wall ultimately depends on your particular items, though, blanket advice can take you only so far.

When it's actually time to pound holes in the wall, enlist the help of a friend with a good eye and lay all your pieces out on the floor or dining room table as you wish to hang them. Measure the overall height and width of the arrangement and the distance between each piece to ensure that you have some consistency. I often leave 4 inches between larger pieces and 2 to 3 inches between smaller ones.

Now, having just said all that about common threads and intentionality, there is a different type of gallery wall to consider: the truly random, eclectic, *collected* wall of things. It's a casual, bohemian look that can be wonderfully excessive—the baby beginnings of maximalism. Such a wall could mix framed artwork, postcards, photographs, ticket stubs, drawings by friends, a string of bells from Bangladesh, and other bits and bobs from your life. I've just described the wall above my teenage daughter's bed, by the way, and I must say that it's delightful. The arrangement is ever-expanding: She started with a cluster of items and has added and added until the objects fill nearly the entire width of the wall. Make sure not all of the items are tiny; the occasional medium-size picture or even a few large posters (again, there must be more than one) will ground the smaller things.

7

ACCESSORIES

Or, how to
finish a room

Styling, or the act of arranging decorative objects, transforms a soulless house or apartment into a warm, interesting home. It can be the most challenging part of a design project, to be honest.

I want my clients' homes to be highly personalized, which means using as many of their own things as possible. Given the recent trend toward decluttering, however, our homes seem to have a shortage of attractive, small to medium-size objects to put on surfaces. And trust me: Surfaces need objects, or they look lonely. If you find yourself short on pretty things to put on tables and shelves, be on the lookout for these items.

TRAYS

I recently put a tray in my daughters' bathroom to corral their innumerable bottles and jars and sprayers. I have one under the liquor bottles in the butler's pantry. I put a tray under the TV remotes. I always need trays for coffee tables and dressers and kitchen counters, and I am looking for one to put on a client's front hall table for keys. Bottom line: You can never have enough trays. When you see one you like, buy it. Have a messy pile of just about anything? Put it all on a tray, and all of a sudden it becomes intentional. "I'm the mail, and I'm meant to be here, because I'm on a *tray*!" (More on this, and other strategies for tackling clutter, in Chapter 8.)

BOWLS

Bowls—especially those 12 inches in diameter or larger—can be extremely useful as decorative accessories. I'm not talking about mixing bowls but *pretty* bowls, such as porcelain, brass, découpage[1]—whatever appeals to you. Like trays, they can go lots of places: on coffee tables, stacks of books, and sideboards, for starters.

If the inside of a bowl is decorated (or if the bowl is on a high shelf), you may leave it empty. If the inside is visible and/or if the bowl isn't very interesting on its own, consider filling a large one with pinecones, wooden apples, orange-and-clove pomander balls (can we bring these back, please?), vintage billiard balls, or the like. Preferably something authentic to you or the area in which you live. (Moss balls are decorator-y and a bit dated, but I do like the punch of green they bring to a room.) If the bowl is small, consider marbles, spools, seashells, or any small items that say something about you. When in doubt, leave a bowl empty. For now.

....

[1] The technique of decorating an object with layered cutouts from magazines or other patterned paper and then varnishing it. To tell you the truth, I never gave it much thought until I saw a client's découpaged stair risers, which are delightful *and* appropriate in the context of her historic house and enthusiasm for vintage objects.

FRAMED PHOTOGRAPHS

Picture frames can be silver, brass, marquetry . . . they just need to be, you know, nice. You may bristle at this request, but I'm going to ask you not to clutter your surfaces with too many family photographs, especially in the living room. Feel free to sprinkle framed pictures throughout a bookcase, or place one horizontal and one vertical picture next to each other on an end table with a smaller object in between. But unless you have a baby grand piano that's crammed with photos of four generations of your family (which can be extremely charming), I advise against too many tabletop photographs in your more public rooms.

BOOKS

First and foremost, books are meant to be read. My husband is extremely proud of the fact that he or I have read every single one of the books on our family room bookshelves (all right, all right, mostly he). There are as many ways to style bookcases as there are ways to hang gallery walls. A few looks predominate.

✦ **Erudite/old money.** (Known at one time as "bookshelf wealth.") Books, books, and more books. Shelves stuffed to the gills. Horizontal books crammed on top of vertical books . . . more is more. Emphasize the messiness by shoving all books to the back of the bookcase to create an uneven face, and then place objects in front of them. Hang paintings on the stiles (the vertical pieces) of the bookcase, thereby blocking access to some sections. Bonus points for stacks of books on the floor in front of the bookcase: You simply cannot house them all, you're so intellectually curious and learned. It's a look.

✦ **Carefully arranged.** A thoughtful mix of vertical and horizontal books, decorative objects, and framed pictures. I like some shelves fully packed with a neat row of books; some with only a few large books stacked horizontally, with or without an object on top; and some shelves filled two-thirds with vertical books with a bookend or small horizontal stack of books at the end. You might place a small object (a tiny vase, a paperweight) on top of the small stack, or, if you use a bookend,

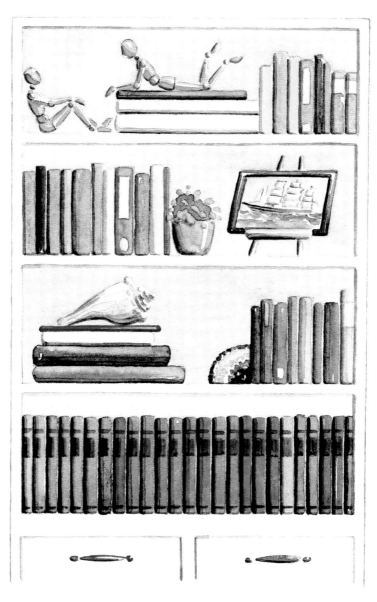

place an object next to it on the bare shelf. The interspersed objects should not be too small unless you have a collection of something, in which case the collected items should be grouped and could occupy an entire shelf at eye level.

✦ **Spare.** I advise against leaving a shelf in a bookcase entirely empty, but spare styling leaves a lot of space between and around objects. A friend of mine arranged the bookcases in her weekend house this way: One shelf displays only a large wooden boat, another has a glass bowl of shells next to a horizontal stack of books, another is filled two-thirds of the way with books next to a large framed picture of her family . . . you get the idea. The effect is lovely and restful.

Books belong not only on shelves, of course; they also are beautiful and useful objects on tables. Two or three hardcovers—normal size, not oversize art books—with a paperweight on top can fill out a lamp table nicely, and it goes without saying that a stack of three coffee-table books looks great on, well, a coffee table.

HOUSEPLANTS

Decorators agree that plants—and trees, for that matter—breathe life into a room. House- and apartment-dwellers, however, agree that plants are a pain in the neck. Or they *can* be, unless you are blessed with sunlight, patience, and a green thumb. The solution: faux plants. They're fabulous accessories, and they've come so far in recent years! It now is possible to find houseplants and trees with silk leaves and realistic brown parts (no horticulturalist, I).

Avoid faux plants with tiny leaves, such as ferns and ficus trees, because they're hard to clean. It's essential that you keep your greenery dust-free by wiping down or vacuuming them occasionally. A faux monstera in a lovely basket fills an empty corner beautifully, and a maranta on a side table makes that surface look full. Faux succulents are everywhere, it seems, but these plants aren't difficult to keep alive, so you might as well try real ones.

I'm not a fan of faux flowers, though. There are few things more disappointing than burying your nose in a peony only to discover that it's an imposter.

QUIRKY OBJECTS

These are the fun objects that don't have a place anywhere else. You can buy them, of course, but chances are you have some already: The Herend polar bear figurine brought by a houseguest. The brass ashtray you found in a junk shop. The artisanal children's toy given as a christening present that you thought was too pretty for your baby to drool on. Display them! If the items are small, place several of them on a tray or together on top of a large book. Tiny objects hoping to serve a decorative purpose work best when tightly grouped.

A Word About Collecting

Apropos of "quirky objects," in addition to providing your family unlimited gift-giving suggestions, collecting gives you a mission when you're wandering through shops on vacation. A collection can be composed of like objects, such as snow globes (I've seen that work, believe it or not), or varied objects on a theme. If you like pigs, for example, an engraving of a sow hung over a carved wooden pig next to three books about animal husbandry equals a collection. One of my favorite examples of a fantastic collection: antique baby scales acquired over time by a client's obstetrician grandfather. Creepy? Not lining the top row of bookcases in the library, they aren't. They look terrific.

PILLOWS

Accent pillows cannot be an afterthought. None of this "Oh, we'll just find some at the end" nonsense. I'm very firm on this. Pillows are an integral part of every design plan, and as such, they must be selected early in the decorating process. I propose custom pillows to my clients at the very first design presentation, right along with upholstery, rug, and wallcovering recommendations.

Pillows not only pull together the colors and patterns in a room, they also set the tone: casual if the pillows are a variety of sizes, patterns, and colors; fancy if they match the window treatments and are adorned with coordinating trim.[2] And of course pillows serve a

[2] Such as a flange, which is a flat, folded piece of fabric sticking out from all sides of the pillow; you may have seen wide flanges on pillow shams. Other fun trims are brush trim (which looks like a caterpillar), tassels, and cording. (Cording isn't that fun, actually; it's just pretty.)

purpose: Your guests adjust them to provide maximum comfort as they settle in on the sofa, martini in hand, for a preprandial tête-à-tête. If that adjustment means tossing the pillow onto the floor, fine!

As for pillows on beds . . . this is highly personal. For those who don't want a bed laden with accent pillows, place one large lumbar pillow (see page 143) in front of the sleeping pillows and call it a day. Other people prefer rows and rows of pillows extending to the middle of the bed. Just remember that whatever is *on* the bed must come *off* when it's time to sleep, so it's nice if the pillows have a place to land, such as a bench or chair.

In years past, many people propped sleeping pillows up against the headboard, which looks pretty only if the pillows are nice and puffy. As with deflated balloons, saggy pillows are unattractive. Instead, lay them flat and place one more decorative pillow in front of them. There are as many pillow sizes and styles as there are stars in the sky, but the pages that follow will cover the most important to know.

Euro Pillows

Euro pillows are 26 inches square. They're huge! And they're for beds only: You can put one on a twin, two on a queen or full, and three on a king. They're not an essential part of a bed's pillowscape,[3] but they provide much-needed height on a bed without a headboard. I tend to lay sleeping pillows flat, stand the Euro pillows in front of them, and place additional decorative pillows in front of those if necessary (it usually is).

Accent Pillows

Eighteen-inch square accent pillows are the most common, and they're practically foolproof. That said, it's better for a pillow to be too large than too small, so I use 20-inch square accent pillows on large sofas and sectionals and on king and queen beds. Pillows that are 16 inches square and smaller were popular decades ago, but they can look puny. The exception is a single "special" small pillow (in needlepoint or a crazy fabric, for example) among the others.

---

[3] I thought I just made up that word to be silly, but then I looked up "pillowscape" and found that it is, in fact, an actual term. Ick.

Lumbar Pillows

These rectangular pillows come in many sizes, and as such are very handy. Small ones can be used on comfy chairs when you don't want to obscure the upholstery, for example. If you're pillow-averse, placing a single large lumbar—say 24 inches wide by 10 inches high—in the center of a sofa is the very least you can get away with in terms of adornment.

Bolsters

These low, tube-like pillows are usually seen on the sides of a shelter-arm settee[4] or in front of square pillows on a bed. They're not used often, so you don't need to waste any brain space on them if you don't want to. (Cute story: I was explaining to Tania, the illustrator of this book, that I wanted to depict a bolster with striped fabric, and she asked, "Longways, or Life Savers?" You can't get more descriptive than that.)

[4] Meaning the arms and back are the same height.

Off-the-Shelf Pillows

Off-the-shelf pillows are everywhere, and that's both good and bad. There is a wide variety of colors, patterns, and styles available. That's good. And they can be inexpensive, so you can change them frequently if you want to (or if you damage one). That's also good. But the broad availability means that the range of quality is *vast*, and that's not so good. A cheap-looking pillow in a painstakingly decorated room can ruin the vibe. You may think I'm being dramatic, but I assure you I am not. Look for the following qualities in off-the-shelf pillows:

+ A removable cover, preferably with a zipper along a seam rather than a flap on the center of the back.

+ The same fabric on the front and back—or at least a pattern on the front and a *color* on the back. When a pillow has a pattern on one side and white or natural fabric on the other, it can look like you ran out of the pretty stuff.

+ A welt[5] or another kind of trim along the seams rather than a "knife-edge," when the fabric is just sewn together like the sides of a shirt. A welt or trim along the seams elevates the pillow.

+ A feather/down insert, or, if allergies are an issue or the pillow is to be used in a particularly damp climate, a polyester fiberfill insert that's smushy, not hard and unyielding.

Custom Pillows

If you have the means, custom pillows are worth the expense. You choose *exactly* the size, fabric, trim on the edge, and additional trim on the face of the pillow if you like. Then there's the type of insert, which I mentioned above; there are myriad combinations of feather and down and different kinds of polyfill available. Custom pillows are truly that: highly customized to make your room look amazing.

---

[5] Also known as piping. There are two types: "self welt" (which uses the same fabric as the pillow) and "contrast welt" (a different fabric).

8

CLUTTER

Coats, shoes, and bags . . .
what to do? What to do?

Clutter has not always been viewed as an interior design issue, but of course it is! I asked several friends what they find most difficult about decorating their homes, and this was one of the most common answers. (Another common decorating obstacle was "my spouse," but there's precious little I can do about that.)

Clutter on surfaces (let's call it "small clutter") is relatively easy to tame, but items near the front door ("large clutter") require a more sophisticated strategy.

SMALL CLUTTER

You'll be astonished how tidy a room looks after reducing, stacking, and straightening have taken place. Your goal is to see the surfaces of your furniture. If you simply have too many of something, such as framed photographs (see page 133), reduce the number. Sort mail and magazines as they come through the door (keep a basket nearby for immediate recycling), and neatly stack the remaining items on a tray, a trick you know from page 131. Place keys in a pretty bowl. Straighten the piles of books.

It should go without saying that everything should have a rightful place, even if it's untraditional. For example, if the dining room is a frequent work-from-home or homework area, place a tray on the table for pens and pencils (in a pretty jar or cup, of course), notepads, a stapler, and other such items. Better yet, dedicate a drawer in the sideboard to office supplies. If you lack storage, consider purchasing a deep rectangular basket or attractive box into which you can pile laptops, notebooks, loose papers, and reading glasses at the end of the day. I do this every weekday evening, and believe me: It's much nicer to pick up a fork at dinner than a stray pair of scissors.

Bedroom surfaces—the tops of dressers and bed-side tables—are particularly clutter-prone. This is why, for the latter, I prefer bedside tables with an open shelf or two and, ideally, a drawer. Even relegating your box of tissues to a shelf looks tidier than keeping it on top of the table, and heaven knows that books look better standing side by side on a shelf than piled on the floor. For charging your electronics overnight, a piece that has a large hole in the back—or better yet, no back at all—is fantastic: Cords pass through easily, and your phone and tablet don't take up space on the table's surface. A drawer next to the bed is a luxury indeed: Pens and notepads have a place to live (if you're a scribbler before sleep, as I am), and your reading glasses aren't perennially being knocked to the floor.

On dressers, corral, corral, corral. Have a bowl for change (is my husband the only person who carries coins these days?), a saucer or shallow dish for loose credit and business cards, a larger tray for cosmetics, cups or jars for makeup brushes . . . you see where I'm going. (The first thing I do in a hotel, as a matter of fact, is place my makeup brushes, eyeliner, and mascara in a glass. If there is a small tray elsewhere in the room—under the coffee mugs, say—I co-opt it for the rest of my makeup. It's remarkably satisfying to unpack toiletries when you know where they're going.)

I have extolled the virtues of trays in previous chapters, but nowhere—*nowhere*—are trays more important than in the kitchen. Clear countertops are a myth; if you cook, you need certain items close at hand, such as olive oil, salt, fancy salt, and a pepper mill. A tray next to the utensil crock (I bet you already have one!) to hold these items is essential. I actually found a plate-sized wooden lazy Susan that works *perfectly* for these items. In another corner, a rectangular wooden tray with tallish sides holds coffee-making supplies. And next to the sink, a small rectangular black marble tray (to contrast with our light countertops) houses the mug with the washing-up sponge, hand soap, and a pretty silver bowl of garlic cloves. None of these trays takes up a lot of counter space. But by herding loose items into defined spots, you create the illusion—nay, the reality!—of order. (You also have made it easier to wipe down your countertops.)

LARGE CLUTTER

And now on to the clutter I hear about the most: coats, shoes, and bags near the front door. If you have a house with a mudroom, a basement entrance, or a back door, you are a lucky duck. Via cubbies and bins and baskets and hooks, you are able to create a space that is 100 percent functional for kids, dogs, and yourself. Who cares how messy it is? But alas! Many apartments and houses are not blessed with a mudroom-like area. Indeed, many do not even have a front hall, let alone a spacious front hall, let alone a spacious front hall with a closet. How to cope?

Coats

We lack a coat closet in the foyer of our 1910 townhouse, so we have a coat tree there, and an out-of-season closet far away. We rotate coats onto the tree every month or so according to the weather and our moods. It's not the tidiest-looking (which is why we're careful not to let too many coats accumulate), but it is incredibly functional. It's *right there*, and even children manage to fling their jackets onto it most of the time.

There are attractive coat stands in a wide range of styles, from contemporary stainless steel to traditional bentwood. Even when the stand is covered with layers of coats, you will be able to see the base and the floor around it, which gives the illusion of space.

A less compelling option for the front entry is a rack of hooks on the wall. Less compelling than *that* is a collection of single hooks. Coat hooks put too many holes in the wall, for one thing, and if you don't install them just right—if you have plaster walls or you miss a stud—they will rip out and you will have to repair the wall (and your wallpaper, of course, if you have any). There simply is no way to maintain any semblance of formality or order once coats are on the wall. Outerwear is not decoration.

If you absolutely cannot stand to have your coats out in the open and you have floor space in the entry but no closet, an attractive armoire—preferably with a mirrored door—could be the solution for you. Beware, though: Even if its dimensions are reasonable (which they won't be, because you need a *minimum* of 20 inches of interior depth to accommodate clothes on hangers), it will *feel* hulking.

Shoes

More and more people are removing their shoes upon entering a home, which is excellent from a cleanliness perspective (less so from a sartorial perspective, if your trousers depend on heels to lift the hem from the floor). Some hosts encourage shoe removal. If you wish to do so, follow in the footsteps of my friend who thoughtfully keeps a giant basket of leather slippers by the front door for guests.

The most obvious solution for a shoe pileup is a multilevel shoe shelf. There are some attractive options available now, but even so, you won't see much of the shelf once it's covered with neat rows of shoes. Shoe shelves with a bench on top can do double duty, of course, but you may not be able to fit more than three pairs if there's only one shelf.

A closed cabinet can be a terrific option for shoe storage, but children (and teenagers, and spouses) will have to be trained to employ it. The effort it takes to open a cabinet door, place shoes on an interior shelf, and close the door is simply too much for some, and shoes end up piled in front of the cabinet. That said, I much prefer real cabinets to the specially made skinny

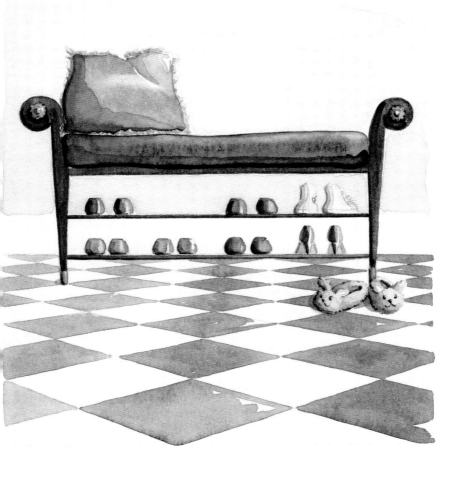

ones with the tilt-out cubby things. Those tend to be too tall and narrow for the top surface to be useful, and they're just so . . . obvious. There's no mistaking shoe cabinets for anything else, and I have yet to see one that's attractive. That said, if you really feel that a tall, skinny specialty cabinet is your only option and you find one that is visually inoffensive, well, there's nothing I can do to prevent you from buying it. If you go the standard cabinet route, please watch the depth: 18 inches or even 16 inches may be too deep for small spaces. It's not extravagant to have a cabinet built to your exact specifications if shoe clutter is your kryptonite.

One client has a front hall that is too narrow for even a shoe shelf, let alone a cabinet. I am proud to say that she and I found a rather ingenious solution. The dining room entrance is to the left as you enter the house, so we placed two cabinets for shoes *in the dining room*. I pointed out the challenge of children and cabinets, but my client assured me that with rigorous training and bribes, the kids will learn to place their shoes where they belong. I believe her. So please consider adjacent rooms if the idea of a closed shoe cabinet appeals to you.

In the "no" column for shoe receptacles: huge baskets and open bins, because only the shoes on the very top will be used. And while some people swear by storage ottomans that can double as benches, the idea of putting newly removed shoes into a lidded container is unappealing to me.

I am not so naïve as to think that these options will fully resolve your shoe clutter issue, Gentle Reader, and for that I am sorry. But there is only so much you can do when space is at a premium. Ideally, only the shoes you wear most often will live near the front door—perhaps your slides for walking the dog, your workout sneakers, and the flats you wear four workdays out of five. For your other shoes, I'm afraid we must develop a new habit: We come in through the front door, remove our shoes, and carry them into the bedroom immediately. Much easier said than done, but with practice, you can do it. I know you can.

Backpacks, Purses, and Briefcases

Bulky and so, so heavy, children's backpacks should never hit the foyer floor. The children should march these behemoths straight to homework central. Their bedroom is the obvious choice. But if they work in the dining room, can you designate a chair in the corner as the place to park the backpack? If the magic happens at the kitchen island, can they be stashed underneath, next to the stools? Backpacks must go *somewhere*, and if seeing them on the floor of your front hall drives you nuts (and believe me, I understand), redirecting the children toward a sanctioned dumping ground is the best option.

Purses and briefcases tend to be better-looking than backpacks, so I don't mind if they stay out in the open. Please get them off the floor if you can, though. If you have anything on which to perch as you put on your shoes—a tiny chair, a small ottoman, a bench—I give you permission to leave your bag on it overnight. A small hall chest or table might be able to handle a modest purse on top, but a briefcase will have to remain on the floor. Lean it against the table (or the wall) purposefully, though. You'd be surprised at what a difference that tiny gesture makes.

THE BOTTOM LINE ABOUT CLUTTER

You live where you live. You're in the home you're in. Tips will take you only so far if you don't have a lot of space.

The trick is coming to terms with what you *can* do, and the first action is to prune. Some of my friends in a small New York apartment have a "one in, one out" rule for clothes: If they purchase a new item, out goes one they already have. Whether or not you adopt so disciplined an approach, please take a hard look at your clothing (and everything, really) and determine what can go. Remember the wise words of English textile designer and poet William Morris: "Have nothing in your house that you do not know to be useful, or believe to be beautiful."

After that, Gentle Reader, we must strive for a certain level of acceptance. Life is messy. Do what you can to clear and control the clutter, and then be thankful for the people who are creating it.

CHEAT SHEET

Helpful numbers to keep close at hand

Furniture

SOFAS	
For small spaces	72 inches (183 cm) wide, maximum, with a narrow depth and low back
For large rooms with high ceilings	84 inches (213 cm) wide, minimum, with a deep seat and tall back

COFFEE TABLES	
Length	18–24 inches (46–61 cm) narrower than your sofa
Height	1–2 inches (2.5–5 cm) lower than the sofa seat
Positioning	14–16 inches (36–41 cm) between the table and sofa

SIDE TABLES	
Height	2–3 inches (6–8 cm) above/below the height of the sofa or chair arm or mattress
Width	18 inches (46 cm) minimum if you intend to put a lamp on it

DINING CHAIRS

Width	20 inches and narrower is safe. But 22 inches and wider requires a large table.
Overall height	32–34 inches (81–86 cm) works anywhere; 40 inches (102 cm) and taller is best in huge rooms.
Seat height	17–20 inches (43–51 cm) is standard. 6 inches (15 cm) is the minimum amount of space you want between the seat and the table apron.
Spacing	10–12 inches (25–31 cm) between chairs, but 6 inches (15 cm) at a minimum.

DINING TABLES *Note the 6-inch (15 cm) increments.*

Table height	28–31 inches (71–79 cm)
Counter height	36 inches (91 cm)
Bar height	42 inches (107 cm)

Lighting

Diameter	18 inches (46 cm) and smaller is appropriate for small rooms or over small dining tables. 24–30 inches (61–76 cm) is appropriate for most dining rooms.
Hanging height	In living rooms, family rooms, and bedrooms, allow *at least* 7½ feet (2.3 m). In dining rooms, 30–33 inches (76–84 cm) above a dining table is standard.

TABLE LAMPS *Heights include shades but not finials.*

10–17 inches (25–43 cm)	Accent lamps on shelves and narrow surfaces
24 inches (61 cm)	Pretty versatile
27–30 inches (69–76 cm)	Good for large rooms
32–34 inches (81–86 cm)	Only for very large rooms and open spaces
Taller than 34 inches (86 cm)	For gigantic rooms with extremely high ceilings

FLOOR LAMPS

48–54 inches (122–137 cm)	Next to a sofa or chair, where a person will be seated
60–72 inches (152–183 cm)	A good standard height
Taller than 72 inches (183 cm)	For large rooms with high ceilings

LIGHT BULBS *Appropriate locations by Kelvin (K)*

2700K	Fairly universal; especially good for bedrooms and living rooms
3000K	Home offices, bathrooms, and foyers
3000K–3500K	Under kitchen cabinets
5000K	Areas where bright light or task lighting is needed, such as kitchens and workshops

WATT CONVERSIONS

2–4W LED	25W incandescent
4–6W LED	40W incandescent
7–10W LED	60W incandescent
10–15W LED	75W incandescent
15–20W LED	100W incandescent
20–30W LED	150W incandescent

Soft Goods

MATTRESSES	
California king	72 inches wide by 84 inches long (183 by 213 cm)
King	76 inches wide by 80 inches long (193 by 203 cm)
Queen	60 inches wide by 80 inches long (152 by 203 cm)
Full/double	54 inches wide by 74 inches long (137 by 188 cm)
Twin	38 inches wide by 75 inches long (97 by 190 cm)
Twin XL	38 inches wide by 80 inches long (97 by 203 cm)

PILLOWS

26-inch (66 cm) square Euro	One on a twin bed, two on a queen or full, three on a king.
20-inch (51 cm) square	For large sofas, sectionals, and beds.
18-inch (46 cm) square	Use anywhere.
16-inch (41 cm) square and smaller	Use only if the pillow is unique or oddly shaped.
Lumbar (rectangular, various sizes)	Use small ones (12–14 inches/ 30–36 cm wide) on lounge chairs; medium (22–24 inches/56–61 cm wide) in the center of a sofa, with or without additional pillows; extra-large (24 inches/61 cm or wider) on a bed.

AFTERWORD
And now, I bid you a fond farewell

Gentle Reader, have I given you enough information so you can go forth and decorate with confidence? I hope so.

At the end of the day, *yours* is the only opinion that matters when it comes to decorating your home. Please remember that rules are made to be broken, and everything I have outlined in this book is meant to assist, not limit, you.

If you feel that you need a professional to help your home reach its full aesthetic and functional potential, *please do not hesitate* to enlist one. Engaging the services of an interior designer/decorator does not mean that you are not creative or stylish or savvy. It means that you are busy, have other priorities right now, and/or are wise enough to leave the nitty-gritty to people who do this on a daily basis.

Your home should be your favorite place in the world. A home that couldn't be anyone else's. A home that makes you happy every time you walk through the door.

Don't we all deserve that? I believe we do.

NOTES

ACKNOWLEDGMENTS

First and foremost, I thank my incredible teachers at Milton Academy, all of whom, regardless of subject area, taught me how to write. (And thank you, Mom and Dad, for making it possible for me to go to Milton in the first place.) There is no better education to be had.

I wouldn't have been able to *consider* writing this book if I didn't have amazing clients, because our projects together have taught me so much. Thank you for trusting my team and me. It is a privilege to work with you.

Sarah Blake was my first reader and loudest cheerleader. It is no exaggeration to say that without her enthusiasm and encouragement (offered sometimes from her unspeakably charming pink kitchen), *Naked* may not have come to be. Thank you.

Fellow writer Terri Sapienza has been supportive in myriad ways that defy definition. *Mwah*, birthday twin!

To my agent, Kim Lindman at Stonesong, and editor, Bridget Monroe Itkin at Artisan: THANK YOU for believing in this project. My sincerest thanks also go to the entire team at Artisan, including Lia Ronnen, Laura Cherkas, Hillary Leary, Sibylle Kazeroid, Julia Perry, Suet Chong, Elissa Santos, Donna Brown, Zach Greenwald, Moira Kerrigan, Theresa Collier, Allison McGeehon, Claudia Fernandez, and especially Rae Ann Spitzenberger.

Speaking of believing, Jason Reynolds and Christine Platt, your heartfelt encouragement came at a critical moment. Thank you so much.

I extend my sincerest thanks to the team at Annie Elliott Design for their professionalism, dedication to our field, and overall awesomeness as I balance design work, writing, and that insatiable beast known as social media. You keep the trains running on time, which is no small feat.

I'm extremely grateful for the professionals who spread the word about my work, especially Sherry Moeller of Moki Media and Paige Knapp and Raeya Swope at Kylee Social. I'm equally grateful for the behind-the-scenes folks who sustain me while I'm doing said work, particularly Sierra Collins, Kimberley Seldon, and my D.C. design colleagues. Without you . . . well, I can't even think about it.

Nor can I imagine this book without the breathtakingly charming illustrations by Tania Lee.

Finally, my family. Georgie and Ruthie, I am so proud of you both. You're my favorite people to be around. I love you, even though you insist upon calling me Annie.

And John. How lucky am I? You're the best husband, father, dog wrangler, boat maneuverer, oyster shucker, and drafts reader a girl could ask for. Plus I can depend on you to laugh at my goofiness, even when the jokes are subpar. Thank you for your unwavering support and for being my biggest fan. The feeling is mutual.

INDEX

ANNIE ELLIOTT has run an interior design firm in Washington, D.C., for more than twenty years. She studied English and art history at the University of Pennsylvania and earned an MA in art history from Williams College. After a career in museum administration, Annie founded bossy color, which later became Annie Elliott Design. Annie's work and insights have appeared in the *New York Times*, the *Wall Street Journal*, the *Washington Post*, and many other print and online publications, and she regularly appears on NBC4 to discuss design matters of great importance. Annie lives in D.C. with her family.

PHOTOGRAPH BY CLAIRE HARVEY